Gender, Truth and State Power

This book is concerned with critically analysing the importance of the status of knowledge in establishing 'truth' about female defendants convicted of murder during the twentieth century. While the abolition of the death penalty in the UK has insured that the impact of this knowledge is no longer one of life and death, modern cases such as that of Sally Clark, whose guilty verdict was eventually overturned, nevertheless demonstrate the devastating impact that those with the power to define the 'truth' still have on the lives of individuals who are unable to construct a dominant truth of their own during their trials.

Using the key themes of truth, gender and power, the book also focuses on agency and rationality in relation to female criminality, masculinity and miscarriages of justice. Challenging official discourse which historically has incorporated entrenched constructions of women who kill as mad, bad or tragic victims, this book argues for the creation of new subject positions and alternative discourses within which female violence can be understood.

Anette Ballinger is a lecturer in Criminology in the School of Social Science and Public Policy, Keele University. This study builds on her previous book *Dead Woman Walking*, winner of the Hart Socio-Legal book prize, 2001.

Gender in Law, Culture, and Society

Series Editor

Martha Albertson Fineman, Emory University School of Law, USA

Gender in Law, Culture, and Society will address key issues and theoretical debates related to gender, culture, and the law. Its titles will advance understanding of the ways in which a society's cultural and legal approaches to gender intersect, clash, and are reconciled or remain in tension. The series will further examine connections between gender and economic and political systems, as well as various other cultural and societal influences on gender construction and presentation, including social and legal consequences that men and women uniquely or differently encounter. Intended for a scholarly readership as well as for courses, its titles will be a mix of single-authored volumes and collections of original essays that will be both pragmatic and theoretical. It will draw from the perspectives of critical and feminist legal theory, as well as other schools of jurisprudence. Interdisciplinary, and international in scope, the series will offer a range of voices speaking to significant questions arising from the study of law in relation to gender, including the very nature of law itself.

Other titles in the series

Sister Wives, Surrogates and Sex Workers: Outlaws by Choice?
Angela Campbell
ISBN 9781409435211

Vulnerability: Reflections on a New Ethical Foundation for Law and Politics
Edited by Martha Albertson Fineman and Anna Grear
ISBN 9781472421623

Exploring Masculinities: Feminist Legal Theory Reflections
Edited by Martha Albertson Fineman and Michael Thomson
ISBN 9781472415110

Feminism, Law, and Religion
Edited by Marie A. Failinger, Elizabeth R. Schiltz and Susan J. Stabile
ISBN 9781409444190

Gender, Truth and State Power

Capitalising on Punishment

Anette Ballinger

Routledge
Taylor & Francis Group
LONDON AND NEW YORK

First published 2016 by Routledge

2 Park Square, Milton Park, Abingdon, Oxfordshire OX14 4RN
52 Vanderbilt Avenue, New York, NY 10017

Routledge is an imprint of the Taylor & Francis Group, an informa business

First issued in paperback 2020

British Library Cataloguing in Publication Data
A catalogue record for this book is available from the British Library

Library of Congress Cataloging in Publication Data
A catalog record for this book has been requested

ISBN: 978-0-7546-7478-8 (hbk)
ISBN: 978-0-367-59636-1 (pbk)

Typeset in Times New Roman
by Swales & Willis Ltd, Exeter, Devon, UK

This book is dedicated to the memory of Niels Daae Pedersen, the bravest person I have known. Peace and love.

Contents

Acknowledgements viii

1 Introduction 1

2 Feminist Epistemologies and the Construction of Alternative Truths 8

3 Subjugated Knowledge, State Power and the Annihilation of Condemned Women: The Case of Louie Calvert 34

4 Infanticide and Child Murder: The 'Leniency versus Harshness' Debate Re-Visited 53

5 A Muted Voice from the Past: The Appeal of Ruth Ellis, 2003 75

6 A Victory for Injustice: Truth, Lies and Expert Knowledge – the Sally Clark Case 97

7 Conclusion 125

References 131
Index 140

Acknowledgements

Thank you to Routledge for showing both interest and confidence in this book from start to finish. In particular, thank you to Alison Kirk and Carolyn Court for their patience and understanding.

Thank you also to National Archive staff in Kew for providing such an excellent service and for patiently dealing with my various queries and requests.

I am indebted to the Fellowship Panel of the Research Institute for Social Science at Keele University for providing the space to carry out some of the research for this book, and to my colleagues in Criminology at Keele University, for their support, generously offered in many different ways. Also thank you to students who have taken my Gender, History and Punishment module over the years, for their input and enthusiasm for the topics covered in this book – they helped to insure that motivation remained high throughout the writing process.

A number of individuals have offered invaluable support during the preparation of this book. In some cases this took a practical form, in others, it came in the form of intellectual stimulation; in many cases both forms were generously available whenever needed. My sincere thanks therefore to Ove Andersen, Alana Barton, Richard Collier, Gerry Condon, Mary Corcoran, Marie Fox, Andrew Henley, Ronnie Lippens, John Locker, Bronwyn Morrison, Keld Nielsen, Birthe and Frank Pedersen, Hans Pedersen, Julie and Nikolaj Pedersen, Inge Poulsen, Kirsten Rasmussen, David Scott, Betsy Stanko, Steve Tombs, Dave Whyte, and Anne Worrall.

A special thank you to Ian Crosher who was there in the beginning. The impact of his personal and intellectual support cannot be overestimated.

Finally, to paraphrase Carl Sagan (1981) – which can only be a good thing – in the vastness of space and immensity of time, it has been my good fortune to have been born on the same planet and in the same epoch as Joe Sim. His intellectual insights and patience, as well as his practical and personal support, have been offered in limitless quantities throughout the preparation of this book.

1 Introduction

This book is about the status of knowledge and the importance of that status when it comes to establishing 'truth' about female defendants convicted of murder, some of whom were executed. The establishment of 'the truth' is arguably the most important aspect of the criminal trial and can have serious consequences for the defendant. It could be a matter of life and death in England and Wales prior to 1965 when the death penalty was still in force. How the criminal trial arrives at 'the truth' is therefore a serious matter worthy of investigation.

In popular and academic discourse statistics have high status in the hierarchy of knowledge and are frequently regarded as having the ability to provide indisputable access to 'truth'. Yet, even 'hard data' such as statistics require deconstruction, reconstruction and analysis before their meaning becomes evident. Statistics utilised in the *Royal Commission on Capital Punishment 1949–1953 Report* indicated that of the 130 women sentenced to death in England and Wales between 1900 and 1950, only 12 were executed. A deconstruction of such official statistics reveals that this apparent leniency towards women sentenced to death hides another statistical fact – women who had killed an adult had *less* chance of being reprieved than a man who had committed this type of murder (Ballinger 2000, 2).

This deconstruction of one set of official statistics highlights a key shortcoming of the 'leniency versus harshness' debate in relation to punishment which has attempted to establish whether women are the recipients of harsher punishment than men, or whether they are the beneficiaries of 'chivalry' as Pollak maintained in 1950, when he argued that the overwhelmingly male-dominated criminal justice personnel felt protective towards female defendants who consequently received lenient punishment compared to men (Allen 1987, 17). Pollak had thus raised the issue of gender difference. Since the 1970s, second-wave feminists have emphasised the over-simplistic nature of Pollak's thesis (Klein 1973; Smart 1976), and have instead produced more complex and sophisticated analyses which document the gendered nature of punishment, hence, moving away from the theoretical and methodological problems associated with a direct comparison between men and women (Edwards 1996; Carlen 2002; Ballinger 2005; 2007). For example, feminist accounts of punishment have focused on 'the differential impact of law on distinct categories of women', a strategy which allows a recognition of other factors such as the *type* or category of woman standing in the dock (Ballinger 2007, 460). The 'double standard' against which criminal women are judged has become an important concept, demonstrating that female defendants are judged not only 'according to the crime they have committed', but also according to their compliance with acceptable discourses around femininity (Ballinger 2007, 460). The social construction of femininity has thus formed an important axis around which existing feminist analysis of punishment has been developed. In particular, it has allowed an analysis which recognises that while women who are able to demonstrate compliance with appropriate feminine behaviour and conduct may benefit from the gendered nature of law, those who fail to conform to acceptable standards of femininity will pay the full punitive price for their deviance: 'Where good women may attract the sympathies of the court, a positively censorious approach may be taken to women who are thought to be bad' (Naffine 1990, 142).

A simplistic 'equity study', relying solely on statistical analysis, such as that found in the *Capital Punishment Report* regarding reprieved women compared to reprieved men, is thus unable to reveal the gendered nature of apparently factual data. That is to say, women who kill adults are perceived to have committed a more serious transgression against femininity compared to – for example – women who commit infanticide, a crime which reinforces dominant discourses around femininity, motherhood and pathology (Morris and Wilczynski 1993).

This book is also about power. The deconstruction of official discourse carries the promise of a revelation of an 'alternative truth' with which to interrogate and critique dominant regimes of truth that may ultimately offer a significant increase in our understanding of gender and punishment. However, as Faith has noted, 'the authority to identify "empirical truths" and to interpret observable, testable "facts" is dependent on existing power relations within given social contexts' (cited in Ballinger 2003, 219). The case-studies analysed in subsequent chapters document the overwhelming power differences between the defendants and those working within the criminal justice system, when it came to constructing the dominant truth about events surrounding both the women and the crimes for which they were found guilty. As a result of the criminal justice system's ability to present itself as neutral, value-free and politically independent (Lacey *et al.* 1990, 152) – the very discourses through which legitimacy for the law is founded – the autobiographical and experiential 'truths' of the condemned could easily be undermined. Yet, it is precisely due to this power and potential of the legal system to have a serious impact upon defendants that those committed to social justice adopt a critical perspective towards official discourse (Gilligan 2004, 12). A theme of the book is therefore the retrieval and excavation of subjugated knowledge for the purpose of generating knowledge from 'below'. The aim of this process is to reconstruct new configurations of 'truth' which allow hitherto silenced groups to speak for themselves, in turn leading to the creation of new spaces for subjugated knowledge to flourish. The importance of this aim cannot be over-estimated, for as Rich has noted: '"Breaking our silences, telling our tales, is not enough" . . . In order to be politically mobilised, this truth must be shared, collectively analysed and strategically deployed in feminist political struggle' (Rich cited in Sawicki 1991, 106).

The development of clearly defined and intellectually robust feminist epistemological perspectives during recent decades has ensured that feminist authors have already experienced considerable success in uncovering subjugated knowledge with which to challenge hitherto dominant regimes of truth, and in turn, developing alternative truths about important historical events ranging from the witch-hunts during the fifteenth, sixteenth and seventeenth centuries (Barstow 1994; Hester 1992, 1998; Purkiss 1996) to women who were executed during the twentieth century (Ballinger 1996; 2000; 2003; 2007; 2012). Feminist epistemology has had a massive impact on research methods as a result of its challenge to the stereotypical 'scientific expert' in pursuit of value-neutrality and objectivity, claiming protection from political interests. 'Feminism is, by definition, a political practice' (Faith 1993, 69), and as such, its epistemology insists that researchers state 'why and how particular research came to be carried out, why and how the researcher came to know what she knows about the research' (Stanley and Wise 1983, 50). Implicit to this insistence is a rejection of the possibility of value-neutrality and objectivity and instead a recognition of the humanity of researchers: 'The kind of people that we are, and how we experience the research all have a crucial impact on what we see, what we do, and how we interpret and construct what is going on' (Stanley and Wise 1983, 50).

Central to this challenge to objective, scientific research is an understanding that the final outcome of a given project will always and inevitably be an interpretation of the available data, which in turn, will always be open to challenge as further knowledge is excavated. Faith has summed up this key aspect of feminist epistemology:

> We cannot . . . presume now or into the future to have arrived at a definitive set of knowledges or understandings . . . But as new materials are produced, ideas can be reconstructed in new configurations of 'truth' which allow for previously silenced groups to name themselves and to describe their own experiences.
>
> (Faith 1993, 9)

Similarly, Cain has outlined how a 'transgressive criminology' can be achieved through one of the feminist epistemological perspectives – standpoint feminism – via deconstruction, reconstruction and theoretical reflexivity. This process is never complete, instead standpoint feminism recognises that the knowledge produced will be influenced by the 'relational and historical site in the social world' which the researcher occupies – hence it will always be a socially constructed product (Cain 1990a, 133). Within this context returning to, and reflecting upon, a past research project in the light of new knowledge being excavated is not only defensible, it is highly desirable – indeed it may be regarded as evidence of standpoint feminism practising what it preaches – continuously engaging in theoretical reflexivity for the purpose of improving the quality of existing knowledge.

The Louie Calvert case analysed in Chapter 6 provides a poignant example of these processes in action. More specifically, it demonstrates that when a particular research project is completed and conclusions have been drawn from available knowledge, feminist epistemology does not claim to have arrived at an immutable 'truth' and does not regard such conclusions as closure of the issue, since the potential for excavating new knowledge always exists, necessitating further theoretical reflexivity. Instead, such conclusions are 'only the end of one act in a timeless play, with no known finish to it, as the next episode in the interplay of discourse unfolds' (Pratt and Gilligan 2004, 9). In the case of Louie Calvert, the 'next episode' took the form of relatively recently released National Archive documents which cast a different light on her case and allowed a new truth to develop since my original analysis of her case in the late 1990s.

Intertwined with the key themes of truth, gender and power, a number of sub-themes will also be addressed, the first of which focuses on the issues of agency and rationality in relation to female criminality. This sub-theme relates to truth and knowledge production, since once official discourse is deconstructed and subjugated knowledge is allowed to appear on the spaces vacated by it, possibilities are also created on which to create new discourses – in this case in relation to agency and rationality – in turn allowing the formulation of a new language with which to understand the actions of the accused, and ultimately contributing towards 'increased justice in sentencing' (Morrissey 2003, 35). An important strand within this sub-theme is the analysis of those cases of violent women that do not easily fit into stereotypical mad/bad or tragic victim categories, labels that have been utilised 'as a strategy for reducing the threat that female agency presents when women kill' (Ballinger 2008; Morrissey 2003, 34; Kennedy 1993, 23; Allen 1987). While portraying female violence as being rooted in madness or an inability to control one's actions may ensure a favourable trial outcome for individual defendants, it comes at the expense of furthering feminism's wider goal of achieving gender equality. This is because an emphasis on women as irrational, pathological and over-emotional creatures, whose crimes are unintentional, 'undermine a concept of women in general as fully fledged moral subjects and responsible agents', in possession of full citizenship on par with men (Morrissey 2003, 35).

Conversely, it is equally important that the development of new discourses of female violence that recognise 'their accountability for their crimes and acknowledgement of their agency' does not result in 'a concomitant increase in their liability for punishment' (Morrissey 2003, 68). This book therefore seeks to strike the difficult balance between on the one hand, recognising that women's violence takes place within the wider context of their structural oppression, social and personal powerlessness, and a reality within which their role 'as primary care-givers for children, men and the aged and the disabled, rarely receive resources, support or acknowledgement, and, on the other hand, that while women perpetrate violence from a different social position to men, there is nevertheless some measure of active choice and agency involved when enacting such violence' (FitzRoy 2001, 13, 14, 12). In short, the book challenges official discourse which historically has incorporated entrenched constructions of women who kill as mad, bad or tragic victims, and instead seeks to create new subject positions and alternative discourses within which female violence can be understood. In doing so, it will follow Gilligan's model for generating new knowledge: 'The challenge regarding official inquiry, truth and criminal justice is to construct analytical models that simultaneously both recognise and deny the power of official discourse without eulogising it as truth' (Gilligan 2004, 23).

A second sub-theme to be addressed is that of masculinity. The social construction and deconstruction of masculinity as well as femininity, and the role they both played in the final outcome of trials of women who were sentenced to death during the twentieth century constitutes an important step towards challenging official discourse around gender and punishment. It will become apparent through the case-studies that issues around masculinity played an important role regardless of whether the defendant was executed or reprieved. Moreover, I shall demonstrate that they continue to do so in the twenty-first century.

The final sub-theme to be examined is that of miscarriage of justice. Arguably the ultimate evidence of state power manifests itself in the criminal justice system's ability to generate miscarriages of justice. The analysis in this book does not subscribe to dominant portrayals of miscarriages of justices as being rare aberrations inevitably rectified by the justice process itself, but instead supports Naughton's argument that the normality of such miscarriages indicates a systemic failure within the legal system to protect the rights of defendants (Naughton 2007). This sub-theme is closely linked to the construction and deconstruction of official discourse due to the fact that the 'symbolic domination of juridical professionals' and scientific experts enables them 'to declare their opinions and theories as if they were facts' (Inglis 2003, 178). The ensuing hierarchy of knowledge and credibility that locates representatives of law and science at the apex of truth-tellers in turn 'limits and controls . . . the production of other alternative, resistant truths' (Inglis 2003, 6). The Sally Clark case, analysed in Chapter 6, provides an example of how these processes operate in relation to gender and miscarriages of justice. The book therefore contributes to this under-researched area, particularly with respect to the relationship between discourses of femininity, expert knowledge and the phallocentric nature of the judiciary.

In order to achieve the above aims, this book will be organised in the following order: Chapter 2 provides a brief history of the development of feminist epistemology generated by second-wave feminism. It also identifies the specific epistemological standpoint from which the book's content is theorised. A major contribution of feminist epistemology has been the identification of the phallocentric nature of culture in general and of law in particular (Smart 1995, 78), which has illuminated 'the way in which specific gendered values have come to dominate' (Smart 1989, 27). In turn, this has had severe consequences as far as power relations are concerned, between those speaking from the standpoint of 'masculinized/authorized knowledge' and those speaking from the standpoint of experiential knowledge (Letherby 2003, 30). A comparison between legal/scientific/expert knowledge and lay knowledge will demonstrate the ability of feminist epistemology to evade dominant discourse and in its place create a new terrain on which the voices of the powerless can be heard.

Chapter 3 draws on National Archive documents, including the handwritten autobiography of one condemned woman – Louie Calvert who was executed in 1926. These documents indicate the ability of criminal justice personnel to disguise the mediation of the defendants' own accounts and thus undermine biographical and experiential truth claims. In doing so, the chapter challenges law's claim to truth, impartiality and objectivity and instead demonstrates that the state's craving for neat resolutions and closure may take priority over the pursuit of discovering the 'facts' of particular cases. The chapter thus illustrates that the very concepts which give the legal process legitimacy – due process and the rule of law – are themselves socially constructed, or 'ideological mystifications' (Box 1983), to the point where unsafe convictions or miscarriages of justice may result.

This chapter thus provides a poignant example of feminist epistemology in action as outlined in Chapter 2, due to the fact that these documents were not available for inspection when I initially researched this case during the 1990s. A prime opportunity has therefore arisen to follow Faith's observations discussed above, regarding the production of new knowledge which provides the opportunity for reconstructing it into new configurations of 'truth', allowing previously silenced groups to 'describe their own experiences' (Faith 1993, 9).

Chapter 4 is concerned with three case-studies of women who killed their own children during the first two decades of the twentieth century. This crime carried the death penalty, yet all convicted women were reprieved since the execution of Louise Masset in 1900 (Ballinger 2000). However, rather than arguing on the terrain of the 'leniency versus harshness' debate, this chapter suggests that such pardons reflected a deep concern by state officials about the legitimacy of the criminal justice system as well as the social order more broadly. Conversely, it is also evident that genuine compassion and humanitarian concern existed for women who had committed this crime out of sheer desperation during an era where no financial support was available for those who had been abandoned by the father of the victim. It was precisely the nature and extent of such concern that threatened the legitimacy of the judiciary, and arguably, played an increasing role in securing reprieves for women found guilty of this crime.

Chapter 5 provides a critical analysis of the Ruth Ellis appeal which took place in 2003. As such this chapter forms an important link between historical and contemporary cases of problematic convictions for she was executed 48 years earlier, in 1955. The chapter argues that, despite considerable progress in gaining formal equality for women during the five decades since the trial, ideological and discursive gains have remained more elusive. Comparisons between legal discourses activated during the trial are made with those that featured in the appeal. This allows continuities to be identified within the legal system during the previous five decades – particularly in relation to the limited subject positions available to women who kill. As such the chapter illustrates the limitations, not only of law itself, but also of the formal equality implemented by it, when it comes to ensuring the structural and ideological changes needed to ensuring substantial equality between the sexes.

Chapter 6 examines the symbiotic relationship between modern law and expert knowledge and the role it played in causing what is arguably one of the most serious miscarriages of justices in contemporary times – that of Sally Clark who was convicted of an entirely fictional crime – the murder of two of her infant sons in 1999. In exploring the issues of miscarriage of justice through this case study, the chapter also raises broader theoretical and political questions concerning the relationship between state power and the role of expert knowledge in the maintenance of a gendered social order in the twenty-first century.

Chapter 7 concludes the book by providing a summary of the key themes and arguments explored. In particular the contents of the book will have demonstrated that regardless of whether female defendants have suffered the death penalty, have been reprieved or have been the victims of a miscarriage of justice, both legal and medical responses to their circumstances have been highly gendered. It also acknowledges the continuing feminist struggle over both knowledge construction and its meaning within the criminal justice system and advocates an ongoing engagement with truth-producers as well as the process of deconstructing official discourses for the purposes of challenging state hegemony.

2 Feminist Epistemologies and the Construction of Alternative Truths

Part I

> Feminists have made a significant contribution to the understanding of the connection between power and knowledge. Feminists have pointed out how, historically, knowledge claims have been intimately tied to relations of dominance and exclusion . . . this . . . has led to debate and discussion within feminism about the nature and status of feminist knowledge. Yet, this debate has added to rather than threatened the value of feminist epistemologies.
>
> (Letherby 2003, 59)

As noted in the Introduction, since the 1970s second-wave feminists have raised a series of significant political and academic questions around the production of knowledge and language within Western culture. Moreover, as indicated by Letherby's evaluation of this contribution above, the diversity of the perspectives that was subsequently developed, has added a richness to the debate which should be welcomed. Dorothy Smith's essay 'A Peculiar Eclipsing' (1978) played a key role in outlining women's exclusion

> from the making of ideology, of knowledge, and of culture [which] means that our experience, our interests, our ways of knowing the world have not been represented in the organisation of our ruling nor in the systematically developed knowledge that has entered into it.
>
> (1987, 18)

As a result of men appearing as representatives

> of the power and authority of the institutionalised structures that govern . . . society . . . [women] have learned to live inside a discourse that is not ours and that expresses and describes a landscape in which we are alienated and that preserves that alienation as integral to its practice.
>
> (Smith 1987, 30, 36)

Spender echoed Smith when she wrote that 'women have been excluded from the production of language, thought and reality', while men's standpoint has been presented as universal and objective (1980, 143), hence ascribed with the authority to define what counts as knowledge in society, 'what is to be valued', and what is to be considered real and unreal (1980, 5).

Thus, by the early 1980s feminists were acutely aware of the importance of the 'politics of naming' – the feminist task of articulating the meanings of feelings and experiences which, as yet, have no name and therefore, technically, do not exist. The struggle to create new discourses and encode language with women's own meanings of their life experiences had begun, and has since been widely regarded as a sustained critique of Enlightenment values and beliefs, particularly through exposing the socially constructed nature of beliefs about women's subordinate status compared to men's, which had hitherto carried the status of uncontestable, scientific 'truth' within research (Letherby 2003; Harding 1990). An important contribution to this critique was made by Stanley and Wise who, in their book *Breaking Out*, focused on the phallocentric nature of research methods by challenging traditional positivists who claimed to produce 'objective' research. Their critique exposed the social sciences as 'sexist, biased and rotten with patriarchal values': 'Masculine ideologies are the creation of masculine subjectivity; they are neither objective, nor value-free' (1983, 12, 49).

An absolute state of objectivity does not exist outside the imagination of the orthodox positivist – instead 'objectivity' has its roots in human experience and action in the same way 'subjectivity' has. Indeed, for Sandra Harding, feminists should question the desire for objectivity with its emphasis on 'laws and calculable results' that contributes to the representation of the researcher as a disembodied, 'invisible, anonymous voice of authority' (1987, 9), which, in turn, has severe implications for power relationships between the researcher and the researched. To reduce power inequality between the two, Stanley and Wise proposed the establishment of a new epistemological and ontological strategy for generating knowledge which avoided portraying the researcher as a detached, omnipotent 'expert on a different critical plane from those' being studied (1993, 7). Instead, of treating the researched as mere objects, feminists would make explicit that the researcher does not hold some special knowledge over those being researched, and indeed, cannot ever know how they experience their reality. Rather, findings would be recognised as a socially constructed interpretation of another person's experience, not an objective, value-free set of facts as had hitherto been claimed by traditional positivist researchers (Stanley and Wise 1983, 170).

Breaking Out constituted a major challenge to established social science research and inspired a rethinking of what constitutes knowledge, how that knowledge is produced, for what purpose and to what use it is put. Crucially, it also presented a coherent and substantial proposal for establishing new epistemological and ontological approaches capable of identifying power relationships between the researcher and the researched, which was also suitable for generating knowledge from 'below' as well as new discourses within which that knowledge could be analysed.

Since the publication of *Breaking Out* different justificatory strategies within feminist epistemology have been developed (Harding 1990, 87). It is not the purpose of this chapter to provide a detailed review of such developments, however, a brief focus on key issues within feminist epistemology is necessary in order to place the following chapters within their appropriate historical and epistemological context.

A comparison between the 'straw-man' of traditional research and the feminist researcher will illuminate some key differences (Cain 1990, 125). This straw-man presents himself as a 'scientific expert' who strives to achieve and maintain the most highly prized goals and values within the knowledge-seeking community: value-neutrality, objectivity, dispassion and disinterest, all justified on the grounds that research must be separated from wider political interests and the social values of the researcher. In contrast, feminism is an overtly political movement which exists to generate social change (Harding 1990, 90). Yet, this highly politicised form of inquiry claims to produce better quality research. This is due to the ability of feminist epistemology to expose the gender-blindness of traditional research. With specific reference to criminological research, Cain argued that 'the criminological gaze does not see maleness: it cannot see or speak gender at all' (Cain 1990, 11). This is why a feminist epistemology should transgress the research methods of the 'straw man': 'Studying women as women, and comparing different groups of women, rather than women and men, takes off the blinkers of the male-as-yardstick and male common sense, so that *new* thoughts can come into the social and criminological worlds' (Cain 1990, 9, original emphasis).

This gender-blindness is also the reason why feminists have provided extensive critiques of research results generated from 'equity' studies as discussed in Chapter 1. A straight comparison between women and men fails to capture 'the social and historical conditions under which distinctions between individuals and/or groups are created, identified as relevant and sustained', and hence, also 'fails to acknowledge, let alone challenge, the use of men's experience as the benchmark for entitlement' (Munro 2007, 134). Additionally, 'equity studies do not enable us to pose the question whether or not even absolutely equal sentence might be unjust' because what is being equalised is left un-analysed (Cain 1990, 2–3). As Fox has observed, 'in practice "equality" tends to mean "like men"' (2000, 334).

While the inclusion of women in criminological research is to be welcomed, the limitations associated with this form of empiricist inquiry are, to a large degree, the result of its failure to express a desire to change the norms and principles of traditional empiricist research itself. Even the feminist empiricist perspective which favours research being carried out 'from the perspective of women' (Letherby 2003, 44) falls within this category because it 'appears to leave intact much of science's self-understanding of the principles of adequate scientific research', and as such, remains the least threatening of the feminist epistemologies (Harding 1987, 183). Consequently, many feminists have focused on developing perspectives which have a different starting point in so far as they reject Enlightenment values in various degrees and instead attempt to carve out their own epistemological priorities. The following section explores the viability of these perspectives.

The Feminist Standpoint versus Postmodern Feminist Debate

A number of authors have argued that feminism is inherently postmodern due to its extensive critique of the Enlightenment legacy with regard to gender relations, phallocentric language and the deeply ingrained notion of 'objective masculine science' (Letherby 2003, 53; Flax 1990; Harding 1990), as discussed above. Moreover, as I have also indicated, feminism has challenged the fundamental Enlightenment discourses surrounding universalising truth-claims – the idea that with the 'correct' application of 'scientific' methods an objective truth is 'out there' waiting to be discovered, independent of politics and social relationships (Holmwood 1995, 420). Feminists have instead insisted that 'knowledge claims are always socially situated, and the failure of dominant groups' such as the 'straw men' discussed above, to 'critically and systematically' interrogate their privileged position and the effect that such a position has on both their personal beliefs as well as their research, ensures that the knowledge generated will always be partial, subjective and open to challenge. Indeed, such research may 'end up legitimating exploitative "practical politics" even when those who produce [it] have good intentions' (Harding in Letherby 2003, 45). Within this context Flax argues that 'as a type of postmodern philosophy feminist theory reveals and contributes to the growing uncertainty within Western intellectual circles about the appropriate grounding and methods for explaining and interpreting human experience' (1990, 41). She further confirms the close relationship between feminism and postmodernism when she notes that: 'Feminist theorists enter into and echo postmodernist discourses as we have begun to deconstruct notions of reason, knowledge, or the self and to reveal the effects of the gender arrangements that lay beneath their neutral and universalising facades' (1990, 42).

Yet, despite the fact there is broad agreement within feminism about the need to challenge phallocentric Enlightenment values and beliefs, a disagreement about the specific form this challenge should take has been prominent within feminist epistemology, and has resulted in two distinct epistemological perspectives being developed – that of standpoint feminism and postmodern feminism. This disagreement has focused upon the way forward for new and alternative forms of knowledge production. The resulting debates have been, and remain detailed, complex and protracted and indeed may never be resolved, nor is it necessarily desirable that they should be, a point to which I return in the conclusion of this section. In what follows, I outline the key points of this debate for the purpose of arriving at a theoretical and epistemological position which will be employed for analytical purposes throughout the remainder of the book.

The Feminist Standpoint

The feminist standpoint is a position which can only be achieved through experience or, by making 'an effortful choice to align' oneself with those being researched, which means it is necessary for the researchers to commit themselves to a specific standpoint – 'to choose to speak as feminists' (Cain 1990, 132). The researcher cannot merely claim to speak from a feminist standpoint – it requires an intellectual and political commitment to do so, which means that knowledge is produced from a specific site and the values and politics held by someone speaking for that site is openly proclaimed and acknowledged. In sharp contrast to traditional research, there is no attempt or desire to strive for so-called objective and neutral knowledge – instead new knowledge arises from the deliberate and direct engagement with feminist politics and values (Smart 1990, 80). These features ensure that the feminist standpoint is particularly well suited to giving voice to the oppressed – it is a method for generating knowledge from 'below' and thus creating an alternative 'truth' to that expounded by those with power and authority (Smart 1990, 80).

Another important feature of standpoint feminism is its ability to give voice to hitherto unnamed experiences, experiences which are already in existence but cannot easily be identified or 'named', since no discourses have yet been created around them. Standpoint feminist researchers can help to identify and name such experiences by ensuring that they share the same site as the researched: 'To produce knowledge for a group of people it is necessary to share their site – to convert your own site into a chosen standpoint for the production of knowledge' (Cain 1993, 88). In doing this, feminism is able to create a new site on which the voices of the powerless, for example the voices of condemned prisoners, can be heard, and, by implication, 'this analytical process also allows feminist epistemology to challenge the social construction of state-defined "truth"' (Ballinger 2003, 220), and thus confront the power inequality between those in privileged positions who construct official discourse and the powerless, frequently at the receiving end of the consequences of such discourses.

Cain has explained how those committed to the feminist standpoint can transgress traditional methods of creating new knowledge by employing a three-stage strategy involving the *de*-construction of state-defined official discourse; the *re*construction of a new, alternative 'truth' from the specific site of standpoint feminism; and, finally, engaging in 'theoretical reflexivity' – a necessary third step before theorising about the difference between official discourse and the newly generated subjugated knowledge can take place (Cain 1990b, 6).

Although standpoint feminism concerns itself with the reconstruction of new knowledge which can be regarded as an alternative 'truth', it avoids the pitfalls of traditional research which strives to uncover an independent, definitive truth as outlined above, by emphasising that even alternative truths will be influenced by the 'relational and historical site in the social world' which the researcher occupies. In short, whatever research method is employed, the new knowledge generated will *always* be a socially constructed product, but, as 'the presence of the researcher as an ordinary human being with the usual complement of human attributes, cannot be avoided' it is better to devise a research method which utilises this presence, than to pretend it does not exist (Stanley and Wise 1983, 150). Moreover, precisely because the consciousness of the researcher is made explicit, a more accurate and better quality knowledge is produced since those examining it are made aware of the context within which it was generated.

Finally, the ability of standpoint feminism to 'evade dominant knowledges' and 'generate new knowledges from repressed common senses' (Cain 1990b, 134–5) is precisely what highlights feminist epistemology's ability to 'directly and far-reachingly challenge non-feminist frameworks and ways of working' (Stanley and Wise 1993, 189).

In sum, standpoint feminism can be understood to stand firmly on the terrain of the postmodern due to its critique of Enlightenment philosophy and its commitment to developing 'new paradigms of social criticism which do not rely on traditional philosophical underpinnings' (Fraser and Nicholson 1990, 19). Its emphasis on deconstruction also reveals postmodern leanings. Yet, it undoubtedly retains aspects of modernism too, particularly with regard to its insistence on maintaining gender as a category. This insistence is rooted in a recognition of women as an oppressed group within heteropatriarchy which has resulted in structural and institutionalised power differences between men and women. In order to address such power differences standpoint feminism emphasises the importance of privileging women's standpoint as well as identifying the common experiences which women share as a result of their oppression (Comack 1999, 295). This is done with a view to make alliances whose ultimate goal is to create social and legal changes that eradicate structural power inequalities between men and women (Cain 1990, 134–5).

This strategy has led to accusations of essentialism from postmodern feminists, but Comack has addressed this critique by maintaining that 'locating women's lives within the nexus of class, race, and gender relations does not, by definition, mean that such categories are taken as "natural" or "pre-given"', and furthermore, having common experiences does not imply having the *same* experiences; instead standpoint feminists advocate turning the *diversity* of women's experiences and understandings of them into 'subjects of investigation' (1999, 295).

Harding too has responded to the postmodern critique of essentialism:

> Standpoint theory does not require any kind of feminine essentialism . . . It analyses the essentialism that androcentrism assigns to women, locates its historical conditions, and proposes ways to counter it. Standpoint theory does not assume that women are different from men in that they are free of participation in race, class, and homophobic social relations. These theorists constantly call for more vigorous feminist analysis of and politics against these forms of oppression.
>
> (1990, 99)

It can thus be seen that standpoint feminists insist on an understanding of women's oppression as being based in materialist as well as discursive structures of power (Comack 1999, 292).

The second modernist strand within standpoint feminism can be observed through its insistence on creating 'better quality knowledge' (Cain cited in Comack 1999, 291) by replacing androcentric knowledge with an alternative 'truth' generated from the feminist standpoint. This focus on generating an alternative truth – and, in its early formulation – the suggestion that the voices of the oppressed were less 'contaminated' or more 'true' than those of the oppressors – together with its insistence on retaining the category of gender – has generated intense levels of critique from postmodern feminists.

Postmodern Feminism

The postmodern starting point is a denial 'that a single and unseamed social as well as physical reality exists "out there", and that particular kinds of persons . . . have a greater degree of access to knowledge of this' (Stanley and Wise 1993, 189). While standpoint feminism and postmodernism are united in rejecting 'one reality which arises from "the falsely universalizing perspective of the master" . . . postmodern feminism does not seek to impose a different unitary reality' (Harding cited in Letherby 2003, 51), but places enormous emphasis on 'differences' between individual subjects. The focus is therefore on fractured subjectivities rather than communality:

> any individual's life is determined by multiple factors which conflict and interlink with each other, producing differential effects . . . against this background of multiple determinants, individuals act upon themselves and order their own lives in numerous variable ways.
>
> (McNay 1992, 64, 65)

However, there is a danger that this emphasis on difference denies the possibility of an alternative truth being generated:

> the aim of feminism ceases to be the establishment of the feminist truth and becomes the deconstruction of truth . . . For postmodernists there is no one truth but many truths, none of which is privileged, and these different truths exist within different discourses.
>
> (Letherby 2003, 52)

Moreover, this emphasis on difference has severe implications for women as a category:

> There is no such thing as the category 'woman', no such thing as a stable, coherent self, no such thing as patriarchy. None of us can speak for 'woman' because no such person exists except within a specific set of relations.
>
> (Letherby 2003, 52)

In short, postmodern feminism is not concerned with creating more accurate or 'better quality' knowledge, but instead focuses on knowledge itself as power, and analyses 'the power effects which claims to truth entail' (Smart 1990, 82).

Postmodern feminism has undoubtedly made an important contribution to feminist epistemology by raising important issues of how power relationships operate – rather than who holds that power. Moreover, its insistence on deconstructing truth, rather than establishing an alternative feminist truth, coupled with its claim that 'there are no overarching truths, no answers, only partial knowledges which are constructed in the specifics of time and place' has ensured that feminists speaking from other standpoints and perspectives must defend their truth claims rigorously and consider the possibility that feminist knowledge too may be only one part of a 'multiplicity of resistances' (Smart in Letherby 2003, 51, 52). Flax notes:

> Postmodern discourses are all deconstructive in that they seek to distance us from and make us sceptical about beliefs concerning truth, knowledge, power, the self, and language that are often taken for granted within and serve as legitimation for contemporary Western culture.
>
> (Flax 1990, 41)

It has also been an important tool for identifying 'a politics of difference' as opposed to emphasising what women have in common. Yet, postmodern feminism presents severe dangers for feminist politics since its quest to identify 'endless difference' makes it increasingly unlikely that it would allow *any* 'determinate generalisations' (Nicholson 1990, 8). Tosh has observed:

> Multivalence and contingency can . . . be overplayed. The virtual absence of 'patriarchy' from the scholarly lexicon at the present time points to a disconcerting shift away from those deep-set and enduring inequalities between men and women which informed scholarly work in the 1970s and 1980s.
>
> (2004, 56)

Thus, just as postmodernists have considered lived experience and material reality inadequate for revealing 'a woman's standpoint', so standpoint feminists have critiqued the limitations of postmodernism's reliance on discourse, which has led to an analysis based solely on women as 'discursively constructed subjects'. In Comack's words: 'there is something more than just discourses at work, and that something may not be captured in the "discursively constructed subject"' (1999, 294). For example, unlike standpoint feminism, postmodern feminism cannot capture experiences which have not yet entered discourse, or as Cain states, extra-discursive aspects of social existence – experiences which fall outside of existing discourses – cannot be articulated (cited in Comack 1999, 294). Furthermore, those discourses already in existence 'are variably available to more and less privileged people and we are not all able to take advantage of them' (Maynard in Letherby 2003, 54). This goes to the very heart of postmodernism's inadequate analysis of power relationships. For example, Ramazanoglu has argued:

> Women's experiences suggest that men can have power that is in a real sense a form of domination backed by force, and that this domination cannot be seen simply as a product of discourse but must also be understood as 'extra-discursive' or relating to wider realities than those of discourse – to other social relations.
>
> (in Letherby 2003, 54)

In short, discourses form only one part of reality, hence, to construct an adequate base for knowledge production it is also necessary to include women's material reality and experiences. However, postmodernism 'offers few clues as to how a substantive feminist research process concerned with actual, living, breathing, thinking, theorising people should proceed at the level of methodology translated into method' (Stanley and Wise in Comack 1999, 295). Put another way, how can feminist politics proceed 'if gender is to be displaced?' Within this context Deveaux maintains that it is necessary to 'assert the existence of' categories such as gender since it is impossible to 'simultaneously resist an identity and mobilise around it for the purpose of empowerment and political action' (1994, 239, 240).

In sum, postmodernism's emphasis on discourse at the expense of lived experience and material reality, and of politics of differences at the expense of structural categories, together with its refusal to privilege any one truth at the expense of foregrounding subjugated knowledge, means that it 'could seriously undermine the political role of feminist research with its focus on gender relations and inequalities' (Letherby 2003, 54). As noted above, feminism is a movement which exists to generate social change in relation to gender inequalities and postmodernism's refusal to allow virtually all forms of generalisations could potentially result in the destruction of the category of gender, the consequences being a descent into relativism as well as 'an ontology of abstract individualism and an abandonment of theory' (Nicholson 1990, 8, 9). Given these 'potentially anti-political and anti-feminist implications of postmodernism . . . we should insist that the theoretical and political dilemmas of difference are well worth pondering', as well as question the usefulness and value of the quest for 'endless difference', if this quest cannot be utilised to facilitate social change (Di Stefano 1990, 77, 78).

In contrast to postmodernism, as noted earlier, standpoint feminism emphasises knowledge production as a political enterprise, its aim not merely being 'to add to the stock of existing knowledge, but to disrupt the limits of "legitimate" knowledge' (Comack 1999, 291). Finally, it is worth remembering that postmodern feminists are themselves members of a privileged group with greater access to knowledge, who have benefited from the very knowledge produced through struggle, a point which prompted Harding to comment that 'perhaps only those who have had access to the benefits of the Enlightenment can afford to "give up" those benefits' (1987, 189). Ultimately, without modernism there would be no postmodernism, and rather than regard the two as polar opposites, it is perhaps more constructive to view the perspectives as existing on a continuum and hence understanding them as being intimately linked and intertwined with each other.

Standpoint Feminism and Postmodern Feminism: A Reconciliation?

Rather than emphasising the differences between standpoint and postmodern feminism Harding suggests that the line between them is not as sharply drawn as these differences suggest. On the contrary, just as she and other authors have drawn attention to the inherent postmodern nature of both feminism in general, and specific aspects of standpoint feminism as discussed above, so she also maintains that postmodern feminists 'subscribe to too many Enlightenment assumptions' (1990, 99). For example, in criticising the desire to create an improved quality of knowledge, postmodernists 'appear to agree with Enlightenment tendencies that all possible science and epistemology . . . must be containable within modern, androcentric, Western, bourgeois forms' (Harding 1990, 99). Yet, other cultures which did not go through the Enlightenment have had their own, culture-specific ways of generating 'sophisticated sciences' and knowledge which is not accounted for by postmodernism and which leads Harding to ask: 'why must desirable forms of science and knowledge be restricted to the dominant ones in the modern West?' Most importantly for the purposes of this discussion, postmodern feminists 'appear to assume that if one gives up the goal of telling one true story about reality, one must also give up trying to tell less false stories. They assume a symmetry between truth and falsity' (1990, 100). Similarly, Letherby argues that the aim of establishing a feminist standpoint is not to generate one *true* story, but to generate opposition to, and critique of, *fake* stories (2003, 57). Thus: 'Feminist inquiry can aim to produce less partial and perverse representations without having to assert the absolute, complete, universal, or eternal adequacy of these representations' (Harding 1990, 100).

Furthermore, standpoint feminism acknowledges that 'we are not speaking of knowledge which is guaranteed to be right or . . . even successful' (Cain 1990, 132).

However, within the context of gross inequality in access to the means necessary to produce knowledge and be heard and understood through dominant discourses, the purpose of standpoint feminism is to ensure that subordinate groups have both access and opportunity to tell their version of the 'truth'. It is ironic that one of the key critiques leveled at standpoint feminism by postmodernists is that the preservation of structural categories will result in exclusion, since standpoint feminism insists it is a perspective developed to ensure *inclusion* of marginalised groups: 'there are as many knowledges as there are people. And it is to deal with precisely this point that the standpoint epistemologies have been developed' (Cain cited in Comack 1999, 290).

This again highlights postmodermism's ambivalent analysis of the material reality of power relations, for as observed above, different social groups do not have equal access to discourses with which to construct their version of the truth, a point confirmed by numerous authors. Inglis, for example, has observed 'the state symbolically dominates society through maintaining a monopoly over the means of producing the truth' (2003, 3). Similarly, discussing one of the most powerless groups within society – prisoners, Davis notes that when their writing – for example in the form of autobiographies – is pitted against official discourse, they have the 'credibility of elves' (2001, 430). At a different level, Worrall has observed that 'members of muted groups, if they wish to communicate, must do so in terms of the dominant modes of expression' (1990, 21). If marginalised groups such as defendants or convicted criminals cannot accomplish this, they become disqualified as speakers and their accounts become muted (Ballinger 2000, 4). It is within this context that standpoint feminist scholars can use their relatively privileged position to engage in the political act of making the knowledge of the powerless visible, to 'put the women's words on paper':

> Giving women a voice, therefore, means quite literally sharing authority with them on the written page. This includes making it clear when they are speaking and giving their words space alongside [the author]. In the process, their accounts or stories – and the differences between them – become visible.
>
> (Comack 1999, 299)

The aim of generating a feminist standpoint is therefore 'neither the imposition of a "different unitary reality" nor a "return to certainty"' (Comack 1999, 299). On the contrary, it is to illuminate choices made, coping strategies implemented, as well as forms of resistance employed by the powerless, such as the condemned female prisoners analysed in the following chapters. Cain has emphasised that identities are not fixed and echoes postmodernists when she talks of 'fractured identities' as well as those aspects which unite the occupants of a particular site. It is possible to acknowledge some notion of structure such as heteropatriarchy and capitalism *and* the existence of fractured identities simultaneously – the existence of one does not eliminate the other – rather, it draws attention to the sheer complexity of social reality. That is precisely why theoretical reflexivity is so important in identifying standpoints:

> [theory] enables us to abstract from the myriad differences between us without denying them, and to reunite around important sameness. In that complex process our theory changes, we redefine it and it gets better. It is only when we try to think more theoretically that we can work out where the fractures that matter are and why and when they matter.
>
> (Cain 1990, 134)

These observations also draw attention to the transitional nature of standpoint feminism – a positive feature since this is what maintains tension within its own theoretical framework – demanding a reflection upon, adjustment of, or accommodation to, changes which it itself has helped to instigate. Indeed, postmodern feminism may also be regarded as transitional and while this feature means that feminist epistemologies have to fight for acceptance within the scientific world, it simultaneously ensures that paternalistic and androcentric epistemologies no longer hold unquestioned authority over research methods, they too now have to justify themselves as a consequence of the development and impact of oppositional feminist-based epistemological perspectives.

It is thus possible to see similarities as well as differences between the specific epistemological perspectives discussed here. Harding maintains that both standpoint and postmodern feminists 'stand with one foot in modernity and the other in the lands beyond', and 'at this moment in history, our feminisms need both Enlightenment and postmodernist agendas' (1990, 100, 101). Letherby too notes that 'many feminists have sympathies with more than one approach' and standpoint and postmodern feminists 'have much to learn from each other's insights and successes' (2003, 58). Indeed, it is unlikely that it would be desirable for one epistemology to achieve hegemony over all others, for, as I have noted, feminists have fought for several decades against male hegemony within the research community which has taught us to wonder just how many different kinds of knowledges are suppressed when only one theory of knowledge is considered legitimate. Within this context it is possible to draw positive rather than negative conclusions from the critical exchanges between supporters of various feminist epistemological perspectives:

> Despite the challenges to the possibility of 'truer' and more complete knowledge, and feminists' increasing awareness of the variety and complexity of women's experience, feminist research has continued. It may be more circumspect in its claims, but a fundamental link remains between listening to what people have to say about their lives and identifying patterns and relationships which expose the operations of power and oppression.
>
> (Scott in Letherby 2003, 59)

In sum, it is as a result of *all* feminist epistemological contributions that traditional social science has found itself in a position where it now too has to justify its research findings. Terms such as objectivity, value-freedom and neutrality are no longer accepted uncritically either within social or natural science following the sustained feminist critique discussed here. Instead, this critique has led to a gradual uncovering of the complexity of both social and political issues within research. It is within this context that the epistemological and theoretical framework employed in the following chapters can be regarded as 'standing with one foot in modernity and the other in the lands beyond'.

The 'Rise' of Intersectionality

Although the term 'intersectionality' entered discourse in 1989, it has gained increasing popularity in the twenty-first century (Yuval-Davis 2006, 193). According to Davis: 'Intersectionality refers to the interaction between gender, race, and other categories of difference in individual lives, social practices, institutional arrangements, and cultural ideologies and the outcomes of these interactions in terms of power' (2008, 68). In terms of its relationship to epistemology, Yuval-Davis adds:

> Epistemologically, intersectionality can be described as a development of feminist standpoint theory which claims, in somewhat different ways, that it is vital to account for the social positioning of the social agent and challenge 'the god-trick of seeing everything from nowhere' (Haraway, 1991, 189) as a cover for and a legitimisation of a hegemonic masculinist 'positivistic' positioning.
>
> (2011, 3–4)

Intersectionality, arguably, has contributed to feminist epistemology by incorporating concerns about 'difference' without destroying the category of gender by claiming to have brought together postmodern feminism and critical feminist theory 'in ways that could not have been envisioned before' (Davis 2008, 73). Yet, as can be seen from Yuval-Davis's reference to standpoint feminism, it appears that writers who engage with this perspective are well aware that it too relies on the earlier epistemological arguments discussed above (see also Yuval-Davis 2006). Arguably, it is therefore unclear how intersectionality differs from these existing epistemological frameworks. While it is true to say that its focus is specifically honed in on 'differential situatedness of different social agents' and the impact this may have on 'different social, economic and political projects' (Yuval-Davis 2011, 4), I have indicated above, that this same focus has also increasingly taken centre stage for standpoint feminists. Take, for example, intersectionality's claim to incorporate difference, or its promise to 'enhance the theorist's reflexivity by allowing her to incorporate her own intersectional location in the production of self-critical and accountable feminist theory' (Davis discussing the work of Lykke 2008, 71). While recognising the importance of such incorporations, it is not apparent how the tools of intersectionality utilised for this purpose differ from Comack's emphasis on 'locating women's lives within the nexus or class, race and gender' outlined above, or from Cain's thesis regarding abstracting 'from the myriad differences between us without denying them' while reuniting 'around important sameness' also discussed earlier (Comack 1990, 295; Cain 1990, 134).

In sum, as Fraser notes, the '"intersectionist" alternative that is so widely accepted today' has its foundation in second-wave feminism, and as such does not represent an epistemic shift with regard to knowledge production, but rather a continuation of the debates analysed above (2013, 214). As a result it is argued in this book that the epistemological framework outlined above remains, not only relevant, but also suitable as an analytical tool, for deconstructing official discourse and reconstructing new knowledge with regard to the case-studies in the following chapters.

The Feminist Challenge to Legal Truth Claims and Expert Knowledge

Following the development of feminist epistemologies a number of authors have been highly successful in generating 'alternative truths' about key issues within both the state and civil society which impact on women's daily lives. With particular reference to criminal women, two such successes are exemplified in the feminist challenge to legal and expert knowledge. Carol Smart has developed an analysis of the phallocentric nature of law and science, and her work provides an example of a highly successful 'marrying' of two of the epistemological perspectives outlined above, for, on the one hand, she has been described as a postmodernist (Comack 1999, 287), since much of her work relies on deconstructionist ideas; yet, on the other, she employs terms such as 'patriarchy', and 'patriarchal relations', indicating her willingness to recognise structural categories based on macro structures of power (Smart 1995, 129, 130). Moreover, her work also incorporates a substantial analysis of masculinity, a subject which early standpoint theory was accused of ignoring (Smart 1990, 81), yet which is crucial to an adequate understanding of gender relations. Smart identified an overlap between law and masculinity, which is explored below. First, however, this chapter is concerned with another strand to this overlap – that of science.

The Science of the Male Expert

Enlightenment philosophy advocated that science is the correct tool for determining whether knowledge is true or false, and that knowledge which can claim to be 'true' will be positioned at the top of the hierarchy of credibility. Hence, claims to 'scientificity' is also a claim to speak the truth, and this 'claim to truth is therefore a claim to deploy power' (Smart 1995, 72). Conversely, knowledge generated outside scientific discourses, such as lived experience, autobiographies, memories, beliefs and opinions, can be silenced, 'subjugated or disqualified'. In short, defining a field as 'science' is to be accredited with speaking the 'truth' and carries the potential to accrue substantial power within a culture which values this above other forms of knowledge (Smart 1995, 73).

As noted above, following the Enlightenment, the key truth-seeking tools within the scientific tool-box became those of reason, rationality, objectivity, value-neutrality, dispassion and disinterest until feminism exposed these features as masculinist in nature. While law is not a science, it is able to construct itself as if it is, setting 'itself apart from and above other discourses in the same way that science does', by claiming to be based in rationality and objectivity and therefore possessing the ability to arrive at the correct interpretation of events, or even having 'direct access to the truth which avoids the problem of human interpretation' (Smart 1995, 73, 74).

Both legal and scientific experts also construct themselves as standing outside the social order as a result of rigorous adherence to 'objective' and 'value-free' scientific methods and procedures as discussed above. In this way they are constructed as appropriate judges to assess, diagnose, recognise 'the normal and abnormal and claim the honour of curing or rehabilitating'. In Foucauldian terms, they have become 'the judges of normality' (1977, 304). Foucault also notes that judges display an 'immense "appetite for medicine" . . . constantly manifested from their appeal to psychiatric experts' (1977, 304), thereby identifying the symbiotic relationship between law and scientific experts whose presence have become virtually institutionalised within the courtroom, particularly in trials involving serious crimes such as murder. Together, and in tandem, law and science thus 'play a key role, not only in the production of official discourse, but also in securing the ongoing reproduction and perpetuation of patriarchal relations' due to the inherently phallocentric nature of both (Ballinger 2005, 68). Within this phallocentric framework 'normality' and 'abnormality' are interpreted through 'a regime of truth' which ensures definitions of these terms appear obvious and commonsensical (Foucault in Gordon 1980, 133). In terms of law, through phallocentric language such as 'the reasonable man' or 'the ordinary person', knowledge claims are made 'without any reliance on supporting evidence, empirical or evidentiary' (O'Donovan 1993, 428) because judges are 'ordained by state law to decide what is beyond reasonable doubt' (Inglis 2003, 172): 'The institutionalised hierarchies and precedents along with the ongoing embodiment of unquestioned orthodoxies "magically enables decisions of judges to appear as neutral and universally true"' (Bourdieu in Inglis 2003, 178).

In terms of expert knowledge, Inglis's observations with regard to psychiatric expertise can be extended to apply to all those claiming medical expertise:

> When a psychiatrist declares that a person is schizophrenic, psychotic or sociopath, he or she is producing truth. We cannot say they are lying. The only recourse to those who disagree with the truth of psychiatry is to resist and challenge its truth . . . But it is difficult to produce an alternative truth that will have the same power as psychiatry in a court of law. Psychiatry has become the recognised expert discourse in the legal field on sanity, madness and personality defects.
>
> (2003, 178)

Both examples illustrate that success in establishing official discourse and dominant truths 'comes from the respect of hierarchy, from reference to sacred texts and people, to being able to talk and give evidence using appropriate language and adopting proper postures and attitudes' (Inglis 2003, 177). They also both confirm Foucault's observation that 'far from preventing knowledge, power produces it' (in Gordon 1980, 59). Hence 'institutions and experts who claim to speak the truth should be treated with wariness and critical reflection' (Inglis 2003, 3), a point which goes to the heart of the modernist/postmodernist debate outlined earlier, for it will be clear from the above examples of legal and scientific knowledge constructions that both have their foundations firmly rooted in the core principle of Enlightenment philosophy described above – that a single, unseamed reality exists '"out there", and that particular kinds of persons (trained, experts, scientists) have a greater degree of access to knowledge of this' (Stanley and Wise 1993, 189). This dominant, modernist conception of truth has been eloquently summarised by Inglis:

> truth corresponds with reality and exists independently of people – facts speak for themselves. This fits in with a layman's notion of scientific truth, that truth is 'experiential and absolute, unconditional and unalterable'. This leads to a 'hard hat' conviction that facts are facts, and sooner or later everyone comes up against reality. Objective reality can be empirically investigated. Statements about the world can be tested. When a crime is committed, people can be questioned in order to find out what really happened.
>
> (2003, 172)

For Foucault, and indeed from the feminist standpoint that is employed in the following chapters, it is precisely this modernist approach to truth production which creates subjugated knowledge. Far from being rooted in reason and rationality, Enlightenment truth production is based on the disqualification of 'minor' knowledge 'in order to promote the centralisation, normalisation and disciplinarisation of dominant knowledges' (Foucault 2004, 288). Moreover, the state and its agencies, such as the criminal justice system, play a crucial role in the maintenance of modernist knowledge production: 'the state . . . dominates symbolically by developing a monopoly over the means of producing and proclaiming the truth. Representatives of the state are thus able to decide whether someone's guilty, criminal, mad or poor' (Inglis 2003, 176).

Once such representatives of the state, for example judges, have determined what is 'true', limits and controls are set on 'the production of other alternative, resistant truths. It limits our ability to reflect critically about what really happened' (Inglis 2003, 6). Thus, while lay people, including defendants in the courtroom, may be given the opportunity to present their version of the truth, by the time their accounts are heard, they will already have gone through a process of mediation by legal personnel and expert witnesses in order to comply with the 'rational' procedures of law:

> the legal process translates everyday experience into legal relevances, it excludes a great deal that might be relevant to the parties, and it makes its judgement on the scripted or tailored account . . . how [parties] are to speak, and how their experience is turned into something the law can digest and process, is a demonstration of the power of law to disqualify alternative accounts.
>
> (Smart 1989, 11, 9)

In sum, this process whereby legal proceedings can ignore 'the personal, communal meaning and logic of what happened, and instead construct a logic and understanding of events which are supplanted by the force of law' (Inglis 2003, 16) is in essence also the process of constructing masculinist official discourse and, in turn, creating subjugated knowledge as the voices which fall outside official discourse are disqualified and silenced. This is not to suggest that law and expert knowledge *conspire* to maintain phallocentric dominance over knowledge production. On the contrary, law can regularly be observed to overrule expert evidence.[1] As Worrall explains:

> dominance does not require the active domination of one group by another nor does it require any one individual's structural position in a society to be constant. It is dependent, rather on a 'sub-group . . . of relevance at any one time' . . . which produces ideas about 'reality' and who is authorised to define it.
>
> (Ardner cited in Worrall 1990, 11)

1 High profile cases include those of Sally Clark, Angela Cannings and Suzanne Holdsworth, all found guilty of murdering young children as a result of expert evidence, and all subsequently released after successful legal challenges to such evidence (see for example *Guardian* 2 May 2008; Batt 2004. See also Ballinger 2005, 68 and Inglis 2003, 181).

Thus, it is the inherent phallocentric characteristics of both, together with the fact that they are 'produced under conditions of patriarchy' which unites them (Smart 1989, 86), rather than a shared desire to participate in 'a rigid system of male domination' (Smart 1995, 130). This is confirmed by Connell who also avoids over-simplistic explanations which brand 'all men as upholders of patriarchy' (in Tosh 2004, 45) in his elaboration on law's ability to maintain its position as prime definer of the dominant truth, what counts as 'knowledge', as well as the social order more generally (Ballinger 2005, 68). Using the example of the rape trial he explains:

> The legal system translates this interested point of view into impersonal procedural norms, defining . . . what must be proven and what is acceptable or convincing evidence. The courts are not patriarchal because they are improperly biased against women, rather they are patriarchal through the way the whole structure of rape law operates. The more objective they are in procedure the more effectively patriarchal they are. The norm of 'legal objectivity' thus becomes an institutionalisation of men's interests.
>
> (1994, 145)

In short, it is too simplistic to conceptualise law, expert knowledge, or indeed the social order within which both are situated, as nothing more than upholders of a patriarchal system of power and powerlessness in which women are perpetual victims. The powerless, such as the condemned women analysed in later chapters, can and do give voice to subjugated knowledge, but the contest over knowledge between such women 'and a largely male judiciary with male definitions and understandings of human behaviour, which are claimed as universal' (O'Donovan 1993, 428), is a profoundly unequal one, as will become apparent through the case-studies. It is within this context that strong truth-producing structural forces such as the legal system and expert knowledge will be deconstructed throughout the case-studies.

Concluding Remarks: Part I

So far, this chapter has documented the significant impact that second-wave feminism has had on traditional epistemology and knowledge production. Moreover, the unresolvable, and often circular, debate concerning sameness, difference and equality has been highlighted. Acknowledging the important contribution that postmodernism has made to 'the politics of difference' Part I nevertheless concludes by sharing Braidotti's view that: 'Whilst knowing that we are not all the same, that there are differences within and among us female subjects . . . we recognise that there are "differences between all of us and the male subject"' (Braidotti in O'Donovan 1993, 434).

With this in mind, Part I has argued for a 'reconciliation' between standpoint and postmodern feminism. The resultant epistemological framework thereafter can be utilised in order to expose the phallocentric nature of both law and science generally, and in particular, the way in which masculinist law and expert knowledge – 'engulfed in the power and prestige of scientific discourses' – are able to 'invalidate, mediate and/or translate the defendant's biographical claims and experiential truth claims into a legal format stipulated by, and acceptable to law' (Ballinger 2005, 66; 2003, 221).

In essence, Part I has focused on the ongoing battle over knowledge production, between feminism and 'a largely male judiciary with male definitions and understanding of human behaviour, which are claimed as universal' (O'Donovan 1993, 428). This battle has not been, and still is not, a battle between equal forces, for, as I have illustrated, 'representations of truth are inextricably intertwined with prevailing sets of power relations' (Gilligan 2004, 20), and feminist discourses still 'lack the social power to realise their versions of knowledge in institutional practices' (Weedon in Smart 1989, 25). Instead, within this 'battle for truth' (Gilligan 2004, 21), women generally, and feminism in particular, are faced with phallocentric law and expert knowledge that, combined or separately, are seeking to *maintain* their power through institutional practice, official discourse and defining what counts as knowledge, all features which, ultimately, play a crucial role in the maintenance of the heteropatriarchal social order. As the case-studies will demonstrate, 'a crucial step in this process involves disqualifying alternative accounts by reinforcing gender stereotypes' (Ballinger 2005, 68). Thus, a key effect of traditional stereotypical mad/bad/victim representations of female criminals has been the undermining of their own experiential accounts (FitzRoy 2001, 11). This has minimised opportunities for the creation of 'alternative truths' about their criminality or indeed innocence, in cases of miscarriages of justice.

It is within this context that the case-studies analysed in this book contribute towards the fight 'to establish authority over . . . [women's] own experiences and words by demanding that their accounts are validated' (Ballinger 2003, 228). Indeed, standpoint feminists would maintain that it has already had a measure of success in achieving this goal through offering 'discursive space from which the individual can resist dominant subject positions' (Weedon in Smart 1989, 25). Moreover, O'Donovan notes that this 'contest over knowledge can be chronicled as a precursor of future legal battles' (1993, 428), because state agencies such as the criminal justice system are unable to control new – and from the state's viewpoint – subversive configurations of meaning generated by the feminist challenge to official discourse, that ultimately may play an important part in manufacturing new oppositional 'forms of legitimacy' which operate contrary to the position that the state seeks to maintain (Gilligan 2004, 19–20). This book seeks to contribute towards such 'subversive' configurations of meaning by excavating subjugated knowledge and generating knowledge from 'below' that can assist in the creation of 'discourses and practices which are not yet there' (Cain 1993, 89).

Part II

The Social Construction of Gender: Masculinity, Law, Agency and Social Order

As noted in the Introduction, two sub-themes are closely intertwined with the power relationships associated with knowledge production and truth telling – those of masculinity and agency. In order to provide an adequate analysis of the case-studies it is necessary to explore these sub-themes in more detail. The remainder of this chapter will therefore focus on an elaboration of these additional aspects of the theoretical framework to be applied to the case-studies.

In Part I it was suggested that early versions of standpoint feminism had paid inadequate attention to issues relating to masculinity. Second-wave feminism genderised the concept of social control by relating its impact to specific discourses within the social construction of femininity such as those of sexuality, domesticity, motherhood and respectability (Smart and Smart 1978; Hutter and Williams 1981). In particular, such work demonstrated the impact that women's compliance with, or rejection of, appropriate feminine conduct in relation to these discourses play in constructing the 'normal' versus 'deviant' woman, and how, in turn, such compliance or rejection become key variables when women come into contact with the criminal justice system – whether as victims or perpetrators (Carlen 1983; Worrall 1990; Ballinger 1996; 2007).

Following the emergence of second-wave feminist literature concerned with these issues, a number of authors began to explore the discourses involved in the social construction of masculinity. For example, Collier (1995b) examined the changing nature of this construction in the wake of the social, economic and cultural changes that came with the Industrial Revolution. Such changes served to emphasise that 'masculinity' should not be understood as a monolithic, self-explanatory concept (Hearn 1996, 203). Instead, it is important to recognise the existence of 'multiple masculinities' (Strange 2003, 311) which 'embody multiple dimensions' (Haywood and Mac an Ghaill 1996, 51). Nonetheless, '"within the broader changes in family structure" that the Industrial Revolution initiated, the masculine ideal was transformed to the "man of law" we still recognise today' (Collier in Ballinger 2007, 462). More specifically, Collier identified the discourses of work and marriage as increasingly crucial to the construction of 'respectable' manhood in the period following the Industrial Revolution (1995b, 209). That is to say, drunkenness, violence and immoral and promiscuous conduct – all regarded as the 'essence of maleness' prior to the Industrial Revolution – now had to be eradicated in favour of 'civilised self-control' in order to comply with the 'prescriptive moral order and gender ideology' that this new mode of production, and its accompanying social order, required to further the prosperity of industrial capitalism (Collier 1995b, 209; Frost 2004, 547).

Collier's account is supported by Hammerton who argues that since the nineteenth century, the manliness of husbands has increasingly been measured according to their marital conduct and breadwinning capacities (1992, 3). For example, if physical assaults against their wives were combined with a failure to adequately maintain their families, they were likely to be regarded as 'monstrous . . . unmanly and cruel' (1992, 48). Revulsion by magistrates against such men increased if they exacerbated this failure to fulfil the role as 'providers and family protectors' by preying 'on their wives' wages' for drink (1992, 48). In contrast, 'responsible masculinity' could be achieved through monogamy and being a 'good provider' who could be relied on to bring home the 'family wage' (Collier

1995a, 218; Clark 2000, 27; Ballinger 2007, 463). Within the context of this new construction of masculinity where 'a man is not the less strong for being gentle' (Springhall 1987, 66), those who continued to rely on violence to assert their power were considered to possess one of the most undesirable masculine characteristics – cowardice – for this new man of reason and law did not rely on brute force to obtain status. Instead, 'honourable manhood' and 'responsible masculinity' could be achieved through self-discipline, self-control and rationality (Collier 1992, 551, 1995b, 208, 209; Ballinger 2007, 463).

Hammerton (1992, 16) and Naffine (1990) both note that the construction of the 'man of law' was profoundly influenced by the values of the emerging middle class during the nineteenth century. It is important to emphasise that this construction did not develop as a result of a patriarchal conspiracy, but was 'the product of a complex interaction between groups and structures whose roots originated within the concerns and interests of the rising middle-class' (Naffine 1990, 101). Hence, this new standard of masculinity distanced itself from both the 'aristocratic masculine values of "gambling, duelling, sporting and sexual prowess"', and the undomesticated 'sexually licentious "dangerous classes"' (Davidhoff and Hall in Collier 1995a, 219).

In sum, a new standard of both masculine and feminine conduct emerged during the nineteenth century, emanating mainly from a new social class – the middle class – which in turn, was itself a product of a new mode of production – that of industrial capitalism. Both men and women began to experience new forms of discipline and regulation to increase compatibility between social arrangements and the new social, economic and political order required by industrial capitalism to ensure continued prosperity. That is, both men and women had to be domesticated to fit into the ideal nuclear family setting – for women this was largely experienced through the 'cult of domesticity' (O'Donovan 1985) which encouraged their confinement to the private sphere. For men it was experienced through 'respectable manliness' which could be achieved through monogamous marriage and providing the 'family wage' (Collier 1995a, 218; Clark 2000, 27).

In short, while second-wave feminism had identified the discourses through which appropriate femininity is constructed and regulated – particularly those of domesticity, motherhood, sexuality and respectability – subsequent literature concerned with the social construction of masculinity had identified a 'most dramatic development' within the social order during the nineteenth century, that male behaviour and masculinity – specifically in relation to work and marriage 'and patriarchy in marriage generally' – also became subject to discipline and regulation (Hammerton 1992, 7), albeit in a very different form to that of femininity. The impact could be observed in criminal trials and will be analysed in the case-studies below.

Implicit to the argument developed so far is the notion that the state plays a key role in producing and re-producing the gendered subject (Smart 1995), and therefore also in maintaining the dominant heteropatriarchal social order (Ballinger 2007). Through his concepts of hegemonic masculinity and emphasised femininity Connell explains that the state is 'the main organiser of the power relations of gender', but like Naffine, emphasises that this organisation does not take either a simplistic or conspiratorial form involving 'futile searches for Patriarch Headquarters' (1994, 148, 146). Instead, his analysis avoids accusations of essentialism by emphasising that patriarchal power is both contradictory and multi-faceted. Furthermore:

> Patriarchy is embedded in procedures, in the state's way of functioning . . . It locates sexual politics in the realm of social action, where it belongs, avoiding speculative reductionism that would explain state action as an emanation of the inner nature of males.
>
> (1996, 146)

Hegemonic masculinity is constructed against emphasised femininity as well as other opposing forms of masculinities, yet it does not seek or require dominance over alternative forms of gendered behaviour as long as hegemonic masculinity is accepted as the desirable norm to which all men should aspire: 'The public face of hegemonic masculinity is not necessarily what powerful men are, but what sustains their power and what large numbers of men are motivated to support' (Connell 1987, 185).

Connell therefore demonstrates the importance of maintaining the interests of hegemonic masculinity rather than the interests of men. Men who fail to accept or behave within the confines of the main characteristics of hegemonic masculinity pose a threat to the gendered social order and risk becoming members of a subordinate groups 'just as surely as women are already' (Ballinger 2007, 464). Here Connell's analysis avoids portraying 'the social order as a unified, overarching, monolithic patriarchy' and instead takes account of the fact that 'the law does not operate solely in the interests of men, just as men do not operate solely in the interests of each other' (Ballinger 2007, 464). This point is supported by Smart who also emphasises that patriarchal relations are not synonymous with 'a rigid system of male domination'. Rather: 'They employ a more fluid system, containing numerous contradictions and employing varying and various mechanisms and strategies in the exercise of power' (1995, 130).

This is because, rather than seeking to dominate subordinate groups, hegemonic masculinity operates to support the production and reproduction of the gendered subject which in turn facilitates the maintenance of the existing heteropatriarchal social order, as the case-studies below illustrate. Through key institutions such as the criminal justice system, the impact of hegemonic masculinity and emphasised femininity become visible. Smart writes that 'both law and masculinity are constituted in discourse and there are significant overlaps in these'. Hence, 'law is not a free-floating entity, it is grounded in patriarchy, as well as in class and ethnic divisions' (1989, 86, 88). Consequently, legal relations are central to the production and reproduction of 'the most secure foundations of patriarchal relations . . . the family and gender divisions' (1995, 129). In short, both men and women are gendered subjects, hence they both 'have their social worlds constructed through patriarchal practices' in order to promote the maintenance of the existing gendered social order

(Cockburn in Haywood and Mac an Ghaill 2003, 30). Thus, the social construction of *both* femininity and masculinity is incorporated into the case-studies below, even though they focus solely on female defendants, because such a strategy avoids *all* women being represented as potential victims and *all* men as potential abusers of patriarchal power (Segal 1990, 260). This analysis also aims to take account of issues around women's agency and resistance, for as both Foucault (1977) and Connell have noted, the use of power will inevitably result in 'strategies of resistance': 'Such an approach acknowledges the reality of power without presenting woman as eternal victim; and insists on the agency of the oppressed without denying the reality of oppression' (Connell 1987, 149). Furthermore, this approach avoids regarding masculinity and femininity as exclusively negative constructions, and instead allows for a recognition that individual women frequently experience the law as working *for* them during those trials that conclude with a sympathetic result (Ballinger 2007; Naffine 1990, 102). Such cases remind us of the dangers of over-generalising women's oppression and instead indicate that phallocentric law also operates on a terrain which includes spaces of ambivalence (Pitch 1995, 65).

This is not to argue that the complex power-relations between masculinity and femininity have been, or are about to be, resolved, as has been suggested by the authors of more recent work. Since Connell's thesis regarding hegemonic masculinity was developed, the concept of post-feminism has gathered increasing attention from the academy thus marking an epistemological break with earlier feminist thought. O'Neill for example, maintains that post-feminism constructs women as already having become the '"beneficiaries" of social change' and this construction has in turn brought with it an intense focus on their 'empowerment', 'choice' and agency, a process which consigns gendered power relationships to the past – as already having been resolved (2014, 3).

Yet a critical analysis of this process reveals that this construction undermines sexual politics, 'converting "empowerment" and "choice" into consumer activities that substitute for political engagement and collective action' (O'Neill 2014, 3). As such, post-feminism represents a 'pernicious form of antifeminism wherein the "taken into accountness" of feminism allows for a more thorough dismantling of feminist politics, at the same time that gender inequalities are renewed and patriarchal norms reinstated' (O'Neill 2014, 3).

With specific reference to masculinity, O'Neill, discusses Anderson's thesis of 'inclusive masculinity', a thesis which he claims is the 'successor to hegemonic masculinity' and which is presented as a '"good news story"', through its claim that there has been a significant decline in homophobia (2014, 5, 7). However, the evidence presented by Anderson to support his thesis is not persuasive. The fact that men can now wear pink jumpers, one-strapped bags and moisturisers without being considered part of the gay community, is hardly evidence that homophobia has been eliminated. On the contrary a more critical analysis might consider such accessories, and more broadly, the increased pressure on men to pay attention to their appearance, as evidence that men, *as well as* women, are now caught up in a superficial consumerism, that ultimately indicates conformity, rather than inclusiveness (O'Neill 2014, 15).

Indeed, rather than representing a successor theory to hegemonic masculinity, the key premise within Anderson's 'inclusive masculinity' theory indicates a fundamental misunderstanding of Connell's thesis, who never argued that homophobia lay at the heart of hegemonic masculinity. Instead he maintained the core of the concepts was built on heterosexuality – an entirely different starting point, which allowed him to develop a complex analysis of its relationship to male subjectivity, as discussed above.

Thus, like post-feminism, 'post-hegemonic masculinity' theories such as 'inclusive masculinity' lack the theoretical insights of the more structural, critical theories in the earlier work explored above, which was distinguished by their focus on power relations and the social order. Rather than representing an epistemic shift that can be utilised to analyse continuity and change, the inclusive masculinity theory relies on an over-simplistic framework that portrays shifting power relationships as forming part of a 'linear, progressive social change' in which the issues that occupied second-wave feminism and hegemonic masculinity studies have already been resolved. Not only does this line of reasoning undermine, or, arguably, erase sexual politics altogether, it also ignores the remarkable capacity of heteropatriarchy to re-invent itself through new forms of oppression, as I shall illustrate in the following chapter.

As noted by Fraser, the last two decades have seen a change of direction in feminist theory, as a consequence of keeping its distance from any 'sort of large-scale theorising' (2013, 227). Yet, as exemplified in the analysis of post-feminism and inclusive masculinity above, some strands of these more recent developments have come at a price, and ultimately represent the return to a conservative strategy that emphasises the individual through discourses of 'personal choice' and 'self-improvement', at the expense of structure and power relations (O'Neill 2014, 4). As such it is a strategy that represents 'new and more complex ways of ensuring that masculine domination is re-instated, and at the same time protected from the possibility of a new feminism' (McRobbie in O'Neill 2014, 4). It is with these issues in mind that the central arguments throughout this book insist on the continued relevance of the epistemological framework and analytical perspectives discussed earlier, and defend the application of both to the case-studies in the following chapters.

Agency, Rationality and Resistance

> Feminism quite legitimately asked men to consider issues of agency, choice, hegemonic masculinity, power, control, responsibility and motives within the behaviour of men as a gendered population. It is reasonable for us to extend such questions to our musing upon women's use of violence. The difficulty, however, is that simple binary explanations for women's violence, simple classifications of instrumental or explosive violence, 'bad', 'sad' or 'mad' women, are not sufficient to assist us in making sense of women's lives, their choices and their use of violence.
>
> (FitzRoy 2001, 27)

> [A]ccounts of agency which rely on a dualism of male dominance and female subordination do not capture adequately the complexities of agency in an era of transformation in gender relations.
>
> (McNay 2000, 11)

As noted in the Introduction, second-wave feminism generated a comprehensive theoretical framework on the subject of 'the double standard' which revealed that criminal women are judged not only according to the crime they have committed, but also according to their compliance with, or rejection of, the discourses of appropriate femininity. An important aspect of this analysis has focused on constructions of the female defendant as either 'bad' – her crime so beyond the pale that she is 'not a human woman but a personification of evil' (Morrissey 2003, 34), or 'mad' or 'tragic victim' – more 'sinned against than sinning' – 'to be pitied rather than punished', driven by emotions and irrationality and therefore cannot be held responsible for her crime (Ballinger 2007; 2005; 2000; 1996; Morrissey 2003; Fox 2000; Lloyd 1995; Wilczynski 1991; Allen 1987).

Furthermore, numerous studies have indicated the existence of a relationship between the type of woman facing the bench and the category through which she is constructed. Those who adhere to the discourses associated with emphasised femininity are more likely to perceived in sympathetic terms, and hence more likely to be constructed through the 'victim' or 'mad' labels than those who reject stereotypical female characteristics (Fox 2000, 330–1; Ballinger 1996; 2000; Worrall 1990; Morris and Wilczynski 1993; Morris 1987; Heidensohn 1986; Edwards 1996; Carlen 1983). Implicitly, therefore, these studies support the above-mentioned contention that it would be a mistake to perceive phallocentric law in purely negative terms. As the case-studies will show, women whose conduct and behaviour matched expectations associated with emphasised femininity, and who were perceived to be victims of circumstances, frequently received a sympathetic hearing, resulting in reduced sentences. However, such 'leniency' towards individual women who complied with the gender stereotype of 'more sinned against than sinning' could only occur as long as others, fitting the polar opposite stereotype – the 'personification of evil' – paid the price in terms of de-humanisation and severe punishment (Morrissey 2003, 34). In short, the utilisation of labels such as mad, bad or victim, can be understood as a mechanism for reducing the threat that female agency poses in women who kill. Morrissey has observed that, regardless of which of the three labels are applied, they all serve to insure that 'understanding of human female criminal agency . . . remains non-existent' (2003, 34). Such labelling thus fails to 'critically engage with the social, personal or geo/political context which may have impacted upon or informed a woman's choice to offend', and therefore does nothing to further our understanding of female violence (FitzRoy 2001, 11). On the contrary, it serves to support and maintain the heteropatriarchal social order, for as Kennedy observes: 'Women are still the glue that cements the family unit, providing cohesion and continuity, and we do not like to admit to the possibility that there is a potential for crime in Everywoman' (1993, 23).

In sum, while strategies which deny female agency may benefit *individual* women in particular trials, they are detrimental to women as a *category*, because an over-emphasis on women's supposed helplessness, passivity, submissiveness and 'victimisation reinforces their inequality and lack of full citizenship' (Ballinger 2007, 475; Morrissey 2003, 25). Whether women are constructed as passive non-agentic, victimised beings – or as out-of-control evil monsters, driven by un-feminine forces and desires, the outcome is the same – rational explanations that women may offer for their criminal behaviour are silenced. Moreover, these constructions reinforce the gendered social order by emphasising the contrast between irrational women and the 'man of law' who, through reason and self-discipline acts as a rational agent. As such, they form a crucial aspect of law's ability to produce and reproduce the gendered subject, indeed, 'the law is actually a gendering strategy *in itself*, producing gendered subjectivities to which certain individuals are tied' (Smart in Morrissey 2003, 33, original emphasis; Fox 2000, 325).

It is within this context that the importance of developing alternative and critical discourses, a new language and a more complex understanding of the motivation, agency and rationality behind women's violence, become apparent. Smart has observed that 'the subject, Woman, is not merely subjugated; she has practiced the agency of constructing her subjectivity as well' (Smart 1992, 7). Thus, as noted in the Introduction, the challenge for feminism is to acknowledge the agency and accountability of women for their violent crimes, without this leading to 'a concomitant increase in their liability for punishment' (Morrissey 2003, 68). This process involves avoiding all the aforementioned stereotypical constructions of femininity, and instead recognising the 'multiple determinants' utilised by individual women 'to act upon themselves and order their own lives in numerous and variable ways' (McNay 1992, 65). As such, it is a strategy which pays close attention to individual case-studies of women's treatment by the criminal justice system, while recognising the broader structure of the heteropatriarchal social order within which the legal system operates.

The need for the development of new discourses around female agency and rationality has assumed a new urgency during recent decades as second-wave feminists have developed increasingly sophisticated analyses of the phallocentric nature of law's development and history. Historically, the legal system has been 'constructed around the advancement of male pursuits and the resolution of male disputes' for obvious reasons – it was developed before women had either legal or substantive rights – when they were officially the legal property of men (Morrissey 2003; Fox 2000; O'Donovan 1985; Ballinger 2005). Consequently, as feminism has continued its advance towards formal and legal equality into the twenty-first century, the chasm between rhetoric and reality in terms of women's legal status versus their actual lived experience as defendants in a court of law, has widened. O'Donovan has noted that 'the language of ordinariness is not open to women' (1993, 432). Instead, law has continued to utilise outdated, structural inequalities built into the legal system, which position women as either 'the other' or as 'special cases', a strategy which exemplifies its 'power to name its own boundaries' (O'Donovan 1993, 432), and to 'impose its definition of events on everyday life' (Smart 1989, 4). Such strategies serve to ensure the continuation, rather than the interruption, of the existing gendered social order, as will be demonstrated through the analysis of Ruth Ellis's appeal. However, 'failure to change carries with it its own risk in terms of legitimacy' (O'Donovan 1993, 434) and the feminist challenge is placing the 'reasonable man of law', as well as law's claim to neutrality and value-freedom, under increasing pressure. This book is intended to make a contribution to that pressure by providing historical and contemporary examples and analysis of how phallocentric law has been able to maintain its position as 'pronouncer of verity' despite the fact that 'legal methods for determining truth' have come from within its own, unscrutinised and unaccountable system (O'Donovan 1993, 431).

Conclusion

Parts I and II of this chapter have provided elaboration of the book's themes and sub-themes outlined in the Introduction. In doing so, it has clarified the epistemological and theoretical framework that will be employed throughout the case-studies. Thus, the analytical framework employed in the remainder of the book seeks to identify the boundary between the agency of individual defendants and the recognition that 'the criminal process not only pronounce upon individuals but are actively involved in shaping the parameters of femininity and masculinity' (Fox 2000, 325). FitzRoy adds:

> We need to develop a different understanding of women's . . . behaviour that is able to acknowledge women's oppression [and] . . . broad social fabric of their everyday lives, but still name women's agency and make women accountable for the violent crimes they choose to commit.
>
> (2001, 26)

Applying a feminist epistemology as outlined above, the next chapter seeks to develop that specific issue through the case-study of Louie Calvert who was executed in 1926.

3 Subjugated Knowledge, State Power and the Annihilation of Condemned Women

The Case of Louie Calvert[1]

As noted in Chapter 2, second-wave feminism has presented a profound challenge to both criminology as a discipline and the theory and practice of the legal system. In this chapter I demonstrate the dual impact of this challenge in relation to the subject of knowledge production via the case-study of Louie Calvert, who was executed in 1926. In doing so I shall incorporate all the themes of this book for the purpose of exposing the manner in which they not only interrelate, but also contribute towards the construction and deconstruction of official discourse.

It will be recalled that feminists have offered critiques of traditional, biologically determined, 'scientific' explanations of female behaviour in general, and their criminality in particular, by emphasising the socially constructed nature of femininity (Smart 1976; Heidensohn 1986; Allen 1987; Ballinger 2005) with a specific focus on the discourses of motherhood, domesticity, respectability and sexuality, which have been exposed as playing a crucial role in defining the 'good' woman – 'someone who by *nature* is maternal, caring, gentle, modest, unselfish and passive' (Ballinger 2007, 67). The Louie Calvert case-study below demonstrates these processes and emphasises how traditional phallocentric knowledge about women can have specific, and immensely detrimental, consequences for female criminals because they are judged according to the double standards outlined in Chapter 1, that is, not only according to their crimes, but also according to their feminine conduct and behaviour. Within this context feminists have identified those women who fail to fulfil gender role expectations and who also break the law as 'doubly deviant' (Smart and Smart 1978, 3; Morris 1987; Naffine 1990; Kennedy 1993; Ballinger 2000): 'the same ideological ingredients that slotted women into sexist stereotypes were essentially present in the contemporary studies of female criminality that also fraudulently claimed to be objective and scientific' (Smart cited in Carrington 2002, 115).

Such theoretical developments profoundly challenged Enlightenment principles of objectivity, value-freedom and political neutrality, particularly in relation to law and science, and instead exposed them as crucial components in the creation

1 Selected parts of this chapter appear in Farrall *et al.* (2011).

of a hierarchy of knowledge dominated by 'experts' – 'judges of normality' – who can lay claim to 'truth' as a consequence of having produced 'scientific' and 'objective' knowledge (Foucault 1977, 304). As noted in Chapter 1, the criminal justice system presents itself and communicates through the very discourses on which legitimacy for the law is founded – neutrality, objectivity, reason and rationality (Lacey *et al.* 1990, 152), thus, holding the promise of establishing 'truth'. However, far from stemming from scientific methods, 'the authority to identify "empirical truths" and to interpret observable, testable "facts" is dependent on existing power relations within given social contexts' (Faith 1993, 9). Furthermore, within the legal system in particular, these claims to 'scientificity' and 'truth' disguise and mystify the subjugation and transformation of the defendant's own accounts (Smart 1989, 11).

In the case of convicted prisoners, such processes are further exacerbated by their construction as 'untruthful and unbelievable' (Pratt and Gilligan 2004, 3). Thus, prisoners' version of 'the truth' is located at the bottom of the hierarchy of knowledge – subjugated, disqualified or 'muted' altogether (Worrall 1990, 21).

This is not to argue that the knowledge of the powerless and the vulnerable – particularly condemned prisoners – should automatically or necessarily occupy a privileged position, or that they should always be regarded as producers of 'true' and accurate versions of events. Drawing on personal experiences and recollections, they will, by their very nature, offer a subjective account, and motivations for writing or proclaiming specific versions of events must be considered. For example, from the viewpoint of a condemned prisoner, proclaiming one's innocence would appear to be a rational strategy. Nonetheless, with these qualifications in mind, Brown and Clare maintain that such documents and accounts can provide valuable insight as well as a challenge to official discourse (2005, 53). Tracing the relationship between criminology and history through prisoners' biographies to the mid-nineteenth century, Brown and Clare discovered a consistency and persistence which, they argue, form a counter-discourse to official truth that makes 'an alternative reading of the identity of the prisoner' possible (2005, 63, 68). Similarly, Inglis argues that although 'they tend to dramatise or romanticise the past', biographies and autobiographies nonetheless 'have a crucial function in telling different stories, creating different perspectives and rewriting history':

> biographies can help link a macro perspective which emphasise the economic, political, social and cultural structure within which individuals live, and personal accounts which reveal the logic of the thinking and practices of people's everyday lives.
>
> (2003, 5)

Moreover, it is worth noting that there are several examples in existence of prisoners' autobiographies being *more* accurate than official state-driven accounts. Recent cases involving miscarriages of justice have demonstrated that a substantial number of convicted prisoners who persistently proclaimed their innocence were being truthful, they were indeed innocent (see for example Cannings 2006; Batt 2004; Rose *et al.* 1997; Conlon 1990).

Thus, given the potential of the legal system to have a serious impact upon defendants – a matter of life and death during an era where the death penalty was implemented – Gilligan argues that for those committed to social justice, it is imperative to deconstruct how truth is 'discovered, socially constructed and disseminated within a context of official discourse' (2004, 21). This point holds special significance for feminists who, as indicated earlier, argue that it is precisely the modernist approach to truth production which creates subjugated knowledge. Thus, while there are 'many competing, complementary or contradictory truths about the same set of social facts as various actors evaluate these facts from perspectives that are premised on their own inherent assumptions or presumptions' (Gilligan 2004, 21), not everyone has equal access to the means of truth production, or indeed *any* access, as the case-study of Louie Calvert below demonstrates.

This is precisely the reason why feminist epistemology – particularly standpoint feminism – has emphasised the importance of retrieving and excavating subjugated knowledge – that is to say, generating knowledge from 'below' in an attempt to ensure the voices of the powerless can be heard. The aim is *not* to generate another 'true' story or 'objective' body of knowledge, for as Foucault notes, subjugated knowledge is already in existence:

> Subjugated knowledges are . . . blocks of historical knowledge that were present in the functional and systematic ensembles, but which were masked, and the critique was able to reveal their existence by using, obviously enough, the tools of scholarship . . . [In] both this scholarly knowledge and the disqualified knowledge people have contained the memory of combats, the very memory that had until then been confined to the margins.
>
> (Foucault 2004, 8)

Within this context the excavation of subjugated knowledge can help to create opposition to, and critique of, *fake* stories through *alternative* knowledge, as outlined in Chapter 2 (Letherby 2003, 57; Harding 1996, 298).

This point has special significance for the data below which have culminated in the Louie Calvert case-study, because it provides both a theoretical and practical example of the process of excavating subjugated knowledge. That is to say, during the 1990s when I first researched this case, all available documents *at that time* were examined in what was then the Public Record Office. Thus, in 1996 I wrote of the Louie Calvert case, that of the 15 women who were executed during the twentieth century in England and Wales, hers was one of the most 'invisible' cases – 'her "muted" condition almost complete' (Ballinger 2000, 131). Less than a decade later, however, documents were available in the National Archives for public inspection,[2] which included her hand-written autobiography. Hence, from a

2 The document referred to in this chapter was released in 2002. Other authors such as Huggett and Berry who attempted to research this case also experienced difficulties and wrote: 'The case of Louie Calvert presented peculiar difficulties, which at first seemed insurmountable . . . we

researcher's viewpoint, she had now moved from being 'muted' and 'invisible' to one of the most vociferous and 'visible' condemned prisoners in the entire study.

This experience thus provides an example of the *process* of knowledge production advocated by feminist epistemologists such as Cain, who has emphasised that this process can never be regarded as complete, and that even alternative 'truths' will be influenced by the 'relational and historical site in the social world' which the researcher occupies, as noted in Chapter 2 (Cain 1990a, 133). Within this context, returning to, and reflecting upon a past research project in the light of new knowledge having been excavated, is not only defensible, it is highly desirable – indeed it may be regarded as a key strength of standpoint feminism which encourages continuous engagement with theoretical reflexivity for the purpose of improving the quality of existing knowledge, or in the words of Faith above, reconstructing 'new configurations of "truth"' (1993, 9).

Thus, in sharp contrast to law's claims to truth which is constructed as scientific, 'unconditional and unalterable' with 'facts speak[ing] for themselves' (Inglis 2003, 172), when standpoint feminists draw conclusions from available knowledge, they do not claim to have arrived at an immutable 'truth', and do not regard such conclusions as closure of the issue since the potential for excavating new knowledge always exists, necessitating further theoretical reflexivity.

In sum, feminist epistemology as applied in the Louie Calvert case-study seeks to confront the power inequality between powerful state institutions such as the criminal justice system which is able to disqualify 'minor' knowledge 'in order to promote the centralisation, normalisation and disciplinarisation of dominant knowledges' (Foucault 2004, 288), and those consigned to the outer margins of knowledge production such as condemned prisoners, whose knowledge has been subjugated. The in-depth analysis of Louie Calvert's autobiography which follows is thus motivated by a desire to retrieve subjugated knowledge in order to increase historical knowledge of resistance and struggle (Sawicki 1991, 57). The aim of this analysis is to develop 'a new site on which the voice of a condemned prisoner can be heard, and in doing so, challenging the social construction of state-defined "truth"', and thus confront the power inequality between those in privileged positions who construct official discourse and the powerless at the receiving end of the consequences of such discourse (Ballinger 2003, 220). The remainder of this chapter will demonstrate how these aims can be achieved by applying Cain's three-stage epistemological strategy, outlined in Chapter 2, to the case of Louie Calvert.

The Construction of Official Discourse: The State's Story

Louie Calvert was in 1926 found guilty and sentenced to death for the murder of Lily Waterhouse – a woman in whose house she had been living for the previous

were fortunate to find people who took part in the case and who remembered this . . . woman. Without their help it would have been impossible to have obtained so much information about an obscure . . . murder' (1956, 10).

three weeks.[3] Official discourse produced by different state servants and agencies of the criminal justice system about Louie displayed little ambiguity about the *type* of woman she was. For example, Home Office personnel described her and the circumstances of her crime in these terms:

> The prisoner . . . has been known as a prostitute of a low type in Leeds for some years. She has also a bad record of theft and housebreaking since she was 15 . . . She has had two illegitimate children aged 9 & 6.
>
> (HO144/6012)

> The prisoner was a bad character and, although the woman she murdered was also a prostitute, she seems to have befriended the prisoner, with the result that the prisoner robbed her while she was alive and then deliberately murdered her for the sake of obtaining the rest of her small possessions. The murder and removal of the goods were carried out with great deliberation.
>
> (HO144/6012)

The Chief Constable of Leeds Police Department echoed Home Office personnel:

> She is a known prostitute of a low class. Although she had worked as a weaver, she had been dismissed from both of her most recent jobs owing to her being a very unsatisfactory worker and time keeper . . . Calvert was not driven to crime through parental neglect. The prisoner is of idle and very dirty habits.
>
> (HO144/6012)

Furthermore, it was suggested that Louie had killed before:

> The prisoner has quite recently made a statement to a wardress who was sitting with her that about two years ago she caused the death of a man with whom she was living as housekeeper by pushing him down some cellar steps.
>
> (HO144/6012)

Those in a position to construct the official 'truth' about Louie Calvert therefore firmly identified her as a woman who had failed to conduct herself according to appropriate discourses around femininity, and hence, as falling within the 'doubly deviant' category outlined above. Other institutions with access to knowledge production, such as the media, were equally condemning. The *News of the World*, for example, described her thus: 'When standing her trial . . . her shifting black eyes were a psychological study. She seemed callous and indifferent, and her hard, sharp-featured face was the face of a wicked woman' (27 June 1926). Indeed, her career as a petty thief and occasional prostitute was confirmed by her 'previous

3 For a detailed account of the Louie Calvert case see Ballinger (2000).

convictions' sheet which indicated that she had accumulated 13 convictions between 1911 and 1925 (HO144/6012).

Ten days prior to her execution Louie was given an exercise book by prison staff:

> to amuse herself with, and she was told she could write what she liked, and that it could not be sent out of the prison. On or about 15.6.26 the prisoner told the matron that she had started writing the history of her life.
>
> (HO144/6012)

She completed her life story on 18 June, and the matron took possession of it before passing it to the prison governor who, after reading it, sent it to the Prison Commissioners with a note which outlined his own interpretation of her account:

> I beg to enclose this history written by the prisoner in question. On p. 26 will be seen what is practically a confession of the crime for which she was sentenced. On p. 17 is the confession of another murder which has already been reported to the commissioners.
>
> (HO144/6012)

On receipt of the book the Prison Commissioners agreed with the governor's interpretation of Louie's account: 'The woman has written "The Story of her life" in prison. In it she confesses to the murder' (HO144/6012). This simplistic portrayal of Louie Calvert as a 'callous', 'wicked woman' and a double murderer quickly acquired the status of official 'truth' and has remained the dominant – possibly the only account – of her personality and crimes for nearly a century. However, through excavating subjugated knowledge in the form of Louie's *Life Story*, written after her conviction, her own account of events regarding her life and her involvement in these two deaths can now be heard and contrasted with the state's version of the 'truth' surrounding the case. The following section therefore employs Cain's first step for generating an 'alternative truth' – the deconstruction of official 'truth' – within the context of newly excavated knowledge from 'below'.

The Retrieval of Subjugated Knowledge: Louie's Story

One central theme in Louie's *Life Story* which reinforces its authentic nature is her frankness about her past behaviour. There is no idealisation or sanitisation of her past in her autobiography, nor indeed did she proclaim her innocence. She did, however, provide a far more complex account of events which makes the case against her considerably more nuanced and ambiguous than that outlined by Home Office personnel. The credibility of her account is further reinforced by the level of self-reflection which she applied to key aspects of her life. Thus, for example, she appeared to agree with the Home Office opinion stated above, that she 'was not driven to crime through parental neglect' or indeed any other mitigating factors when she wrote:

> I had a very good school mistress and she taught me many things that was beneficial for me and at home I was taught . . . to say my prayers at my Mothers knee . . . Ours was a good Christian home and father always used to read prayers . . . We were sent to Sunday school and had to go to church both morning and night. I was quite happy and contented with my surroundings and Mother never knew a moments worry from any of us.
>
> (Calvert 1926 in HO144/6012)[4]

She provided a frank account of her criminal past, including her participation in a prison riot:

> I went to work in the laundry and . . . I hated washing so I was often in trouble and one day I was that fed up with Officer saying do this and do that – I burnt some very delicate work with a red hot iron and of course I was reported well that night me and three of the girls . . . had a real smash up and we were all taken down to the punishment cells in the Kneebricks and I was put in the straight jacket for striking an officer . . . given three days bread and water and seven days close confinement and lost some of my remission and not allowed to write home for two months . . . and while on punishment . . . was taken to hospital with pneumonia and of course that learnt me a lesson I never went into punishment again.
>
> (Calvert 1926 in HO144/6012)

Upon release Louie went into domestic service and for about three weeks 'all went well':

> then the daring spirit was in me and I robbed my employer of £50 and ran away to Blackpool where I had a good time and enjoyed myself for a month on the proceeds when I came back I was sent back to the Borstall to finish my time.
>
> (Calvert 1926 in HO144/6012)

Although gaining lawful employment upon release, when her prison record was discovered she was dismissed and consequently found it impossible to obtain employment elsewhere as a result of her criminal past. She then 'got into bad company', further criminal activity and imprisonment. One spell in prison turned out to be 'a hard sentence . . . because I was confined whilst in doing my sentence of my little girl'. Louie reflected upon her situation: 'You would have thought that this would have made me different – but no – I had got past that, and prison did not bother me . . . the love of daring and adventure was in me' (Calvert 1926 in HO144/6012).

4 All quotes are direct reproductions of words, style, grammar and spelling as they appear in HO144/6012.

Upon release Louie left her baby in the care of her mother and displayed a disarming honesty regarding her attitude towards motherhood:

> I used to send Mother £1 every week and clothes but never bothered to go home and see her . . . once or twice I would write and ask how my baby was going on but that was all[.] I never bothered about her.
>
> (Calvert 1926 in HO144/6012)

Yet, after an encounter with the Salvation Army she made up her mind 'to be different' and became housekeeper to John Frobisher – the man whose murder she supposedly had confessed to – according to official accounts. Frobisher was a widower who initially was 'very good' to her and her second child, Kenneth, but after 12 months:

> He came home quite drunk and behaving in a disgusting manner and using foul language in front of the baby and when I told him to stop it he struck me when I started fighting back and struck him a foul blow which caused him to fall down the cellar steps and break his neck it was brought in as accidental death.
>
> (Calvert 1926 in HO144/6012)

While recognising the term 'domestic violence' had not yet entered official or popular discourse in 1926, this is nonetheless a powerful example of an issue which the *defendant* considered relevant to the case compared to the criminal justice workers, every one of whom failed to make a single reference to the wider context within which Frobisher died, but merely interpreted her words as a 'confession'. It is therefore an illustration of Smart's observation above, of the restricted ways in which parties are allowed to speak, and how their experience is turned into something the law can digest and process, thus demonstrating 'the power of law to disqualify alternative accounts'. What is left *unsaid* may be as important as what is *said* – both components play a part in creating subjugated knowledge. In this example, only those parts of Louie's account which were *consistent* with the dominant truth about her as a 'bad person' were selected for comment, thus strengthening the case against her.

Louie's account of the circumstances around the death of Lily Waterhouse was also considerably more complex than a simple confession. Journalistic accounts have consistently described Louie's husband, Arthur, as meek and naïve for putting up with her lies and criminal activities (Huggett and Berry 1956). Her account of life with Arthur illustrates a very different side to his personality. For example, he beat her son Kenneth so badly that he was hospitalised. Hospital staff reported Arthur to the 'cruelty officer' and he was subsequently sentenced to '3 months hard labour'. When he was released he became a nightwatchman for four months – the only time he was in paid employment. Consequently the family lived in extreme poverty:

> I had to go out and get the money by fair means if I could and if not by foul at last I got that fed up with the way we were living and him constantly fighting and drinking that I left home . . . I got into the company of the young woman with whose death I am charged . . . we used to go out at night and visit the public houses with the intention of get old [*sic*] of any man who had money and get them drunk then rob them of whatever money they had left and leave them and the last Sunday I was there this woman brought a man home supposed to be a soldier from Becketts Park hospital for wounded soldiers and after he had been there a few days we began to quarrel about him she wanted him and he wanted me but I wanted neither I wanted to leave them and go home again as it was beginning to get a little bit to [*sic*] hot the detectives were on our tracks and we could not go out with them pulling up and getting us fined well on the Wednesday night the day I was going to leave her we went out and had a few drinks with this man and he fetched half a dozen pint bottles of beer and stout home and when we had been home about half an hour we all started to quarrel and it got to fighting oh the drink it is the ruination of everything for we do lots of things in drink and temper that we are most sorry for after well he said something nasty to her and she landed out with her fist at him and they both rolled on the floor when she got up and struck out again I picked up the poker which happened to be the nearest thing to me and my intention was to strike the man and make him leave of hitting her but instead it struck her on the head through him dodgeing [*sic*] out of the road and she fell dead at our feet he went mad then and got hold of her belt strangled her and carried her upstairs I got out and got home God knows how I did it I don't.
>
> (Calvert 1926 in HO144/6012)

Louie's account of events is noteworthy for its specificity about the man alleged to be present, its frankness regarding the women's criminal intentions and her admittance to accidentally injuring Lily – a very different crime from the premeditated, 'deliberate' and 'cruel' murder described in Home Office communications. Thus, it is hardly a statement which can be described as a 'confession to murder', but as with Louie's account of Frobisher's death, the Home Office interpretation of her account of Lily's death emphasised those parts of her story which were consistent with official discourse and marginalised those parts which provided a wider context of events and which stood as a direct challenge to her conviction and punishment. This point is further reinforced by a third example – the misrepresentation of Louie's words within her petition for a reprieve. She wrote:

> I know that I deserve to die yet why should I have to bear the brunt of the whole crime on my shoulders and the man who is responsible for this and who did the worst be allowed to go free[.] I have not waited five weeks under conviction without realising the position I am now in[.] I have prayed earnestly about it and I am truly sorry for the wrong that I have done.
>
> (Calvert 1926 in HO144/6012)

Expressing guilt or regret at Lily's death is *not* the same as making a confession and her words are entirely consistent with her account of having hit Lily accidentally during the fight described in her *Life Story*. Yet, the Home Office Minutes noted: 'She admits her guilt'[5] (HO144/6012).

Finally, Carlen's concept of 'judicial misogyny' was activated by presenting a negative interpretation of events in Louie's life not directly relevant to the case, but which nevertheless served to strengthen the image of her as 'a very bad character'. For example, while Home Office personnel claimed Louie had been dismissed from her jobs 'owing to her being a very unsatisfactory worker and time-keeper', Louie wrote that 'I fell out of work through the mill closing down and slack trade' (HO144/6012). While the exact details surrounding Louie's unemployment is likely to remain a matter for speculation, it is noteworthy that the case took place in the year of the General Strike, a period of severe unemployment and depression. Her explanation is therefore not beyond the bounds of possibility and is not disputed within Home Office documents.

With regard to the Home Office's claim that Louie was the mother of 'two illegitimate children', once again Louie's own account is more complex, stating that at the time of the children's birth she *believed* herself to be married: 'My husband was in the regulars and we lived in the married quarters . . . till my husband went out to France.' After being home on leave:

> My husband went back this time to India where he met with a fatal accident and died the Friday has [*sic*] my son was born on the Friday following now when my boy was three months old I was sent to prison again for six months and whilst there I found out that I was not married as Jim had already a wife living at the time he had married me it was so hard because he had been so good to me and I could not realise it to be true.
>
> (Calvert 1926 in HO144/6012)

Home Office personnel did not dispute this part of Louie's story either; however, reducing it to the simplistic statement that she had 'two illegitimate children' during an era where illegitimacy carried severe moral judgement, served to further reinforce the image of Louie being of 'very bad character'. Having thus contributed to the assassination of her character, state servants were able to present personal opinions as if they were facts, for example, by claiming that 'the murder and the removal of goods were carried out with great deliberation'. While it is beyond dispute that Louie stole Lily's belongings after her death, being a thief does not prove she was also a murderer, and in a case relying solely on circumstantial evidence, no such evidence can prove whether the murder was deliberate or accidental, or whether the theft was an act of opportunistic burglary or carried out 'with great deliberation'.

5 There are many other examples of condemned female prisoners expressing guilt or regret over the murder victim whose words were misrepresented as a confession by the Home Office. See for example the case of Louise Masset in Ballinger (2000).

In the following section I explore the plausibility and credibility of Louie's 'alternative truth' about events compared to that of state-defined 'truth'. This will involve employing the second stage of Cain's epistemological strategy for knowledge production by accompanying the deconstruction of official discourse with a *re*construction of the newly excavated knowledge outlined above, generated from the specific site of standpoint feminism.

Reconstructing Subjugated Knowledge: The Creation of an 'Alternative Truth'

As noted above, despite having been told that whatever 'she wrote could not leave the prison', the matron passed Louie's *Life Story* on to the governor who passed it on to the Prison Commissioners, who forwarded it to the Home Office where advisers to the Secretary of State now had only five days before the scheduled execution in which to consider its implications. After receiving Louie's *Life Story* the response of Home Office personnel was that 'the prisoner could have told this story in Court but did not give evidence' (HO144/6012). This statement serves as a powerful example of the false equality imposed upon defendants within the courtroom, who statistically – then as now – were more likely to belong to a lower social class than members of the legal profession, yet were (and are) nonetheless credited with possessing equal knowledge of courtroom protocol and procedure.[6] Carlen has described 'the judicial rhetoric of an adversary justice where . . . both prosecution and defence stand as equals before the law' as 'absurd':

> the ideal of adversary justice is subjugated to an organisational efficiency in whose service body-movement and body-representation are carefully circumscribed and regulated, bewilderment and embarrassment openly fostered and aggravated, uncertainty coolly observed and manipulated.
>
> (1976, 20)

Louie's lack of expertise in courtroom protocol was exemplified by a much cited incident involving her sudden exchange of 'hat for a more fashionable and expensive-looking one' whilst sitting in the dock (Ballinger 2000, 138–9; *Evening News* 14 April 1926; *News of the World* 18 April 1926). It may have been due to precisely such behaviour – stemming from the context of her status as an uneducated, petty criminal and penniless prostitute from the lowest social class, that she was advised *against* giving evidence by her counsel. Yet, as with other capital cases during the first half of the twentieth century, the non-appearance of defendants in the witness-box could reflect negatively on them and invariably carried implications

6 It can also be seen as an example of an unintended consequence of the 1898 Criminal Evidence Act which in theory should be welcomed, yet, in practice created a new set of value-judgements with regard to prisoners who did not give evidence on their own behalf, who were now frequently regarded with suspicion and more likely to be guilty (see for example Ballinger 2000, 266).

of guilt (Ballinger 2000, 266).[7] Meanwhile, Home Office communications contain no critique of the role Louie's counsel would have played in the decision as to whether she should give evidence on her own behalf, or why he did not argue her case more convincingly. Within this context, Inglis has argued that: 'Being able to survive and operate successfully in the legal field depends on a number of factors not least of which are experience, social class background, and access to good advice and legal counsel' (2003, 188).

Yet, as with the interpretation of her *Life Story*, Louie was once again judged outside a wider context, with the comments made regarding her failure to give evidence revealing a taken for granted assumption that she would understand the best way to present herself and her evidence in court, despite her status as a destitute prostitute with little or no knowledge of legal codes. Thus, the vast social and educational gulf, generated by deep-rooted class and gender divisions which existed between judges, barristers, Home Office personnel – and in 1926, also juries – and the defendant, was simply ignored. As noted by Inglis, 'ignorance of the law is no excuse for citizens of the state. But . . . those who have no familiarity with the law . . . can be easily manipulated if not made fools of' (2003, 188). This is because:

> The law operates within the 'juridical' field with its own language, discourse and practices . . . The juridical field has its own distinctive habitus – that is, its own preordained, unquestioned ways of thinking and acting which become second nature to regular participants . . . Success comes from . . . being able to talk and give evidence using appropriate language and adopting proper postures and attitudes.
>
> (2003, 177)

In Louie's case, this wider social and educational context, and the inevitable power relationships involved were rendered 'invisible' – within Home Office communications. Instead, her ignorance became interpreted as a *deliberate* attempt to deceive, once again reinforcing her status as a disreputable person.

With specific reference to Louie's account of a man's presence in Lily's house and his involvement in her murder, another Home Office worker stated that 'this

7 In his summing-up, the judge observed: 'Of course it has not escaped your attention that the prisoner has not thought fit to give evidence. Well of course she is entitled to take that course. She need not give evidence if she does not want to do it, the learned counsel has said there were reasons of health or nerves which induced her or her advisers to come to the decision that she should not give evidence . . . but when you have a difficult incident like that to explain, it certainly would have been – if there is an explanation – a very desirable thing that in a case of this sort, a case of this importance, especially to a prisoner, that she should place herself in a position in order to give her explanation. You will bear the fact in mind that you are left with this incident . . . and from the point of view of the prisoner, you have no explanation' (Trial transcript HO144/6012, 83). This statement suggests that a less favourable view was taken of prisoners who declined to give evidence on their own behalf.

is the first time the prisoner has told this story'. The inaccuracy of this statement is supported by the Home Office documents themselves. For example, one memo stated that the prosecutor, Mr Lowenthal:

> had F. Crabtree ready in C[our]t with all evi[dence] as to his alibi but there was no justification for calling him as there was a mere suggestion that some-one other than & stronger than the pr[isomer] might have killed the woman in the kitchen and carried her upstairs. Mr Lowenthal was quite satisfied that the verdict was right.
>
> (HO144/6012)

It is unsurprising that Mr Lowenthal was satisfied with the verdict as he was the *prosecutor* in the case. More surprising however, is the fact that Mr Lowenthal had this man waiting to be called as a witness in the court, which begs the question why Home Office personnel claimed never to have heard Louie's story before. In fact, the same memo demonstrates knowledge of Fred Crabtree's existence from the very beginning of the investigation:

> The police, when they visited Calvert . . . *the day after the murder*, had found in a handbag a paper with the [Canadian] address of a man called Crabtree . . . and . . . careful inquiry was made as regards the movements of a miner named Frederick Crabtree . . . This man was in fact an out-patient at Becketts Park Hospital.
>
> (HO144/6012, emphasis added)

Furthermore, Lily's next-door neighbour, Emily Clayton, testified at Louie's trial that 'the previous Sunday' a man had come to her 'house and asked for Mrs Waterhouse':

> Mr Chapple: Could you describe the man?
>
> He was tall . . . He looked to be well built, and he said he was in Becketts Park Hospital, and he was going back to Canada the same week.
>
> (Trial transcript, HO144/6012, 18)

It would appear that the trial judge, Mr Justice Wright, was aware of the potential significance of Emily's testimony for he referred to it in his 'Judge's Notes': 'On the Sunday about 9 a man came to my house and asked for Mrs Waterhouse. He . . . said he came from Beketts Park Hospital and was going to Canada the next month' (HO144/6012). The 'Judge's Notes' also referred to Detective Officer Chester's testimony that he had found 'papers with [the Canadian] address of man called Crabtree' in Louie's handbag when she was first interviewed. Finally, providing indisputable proof that Louie had discussed Fred Crabtree the very first time she was interviewed by police, the judge noted Detective Superintendent Pass's statement, taken the day after Lily's body was found, where he testified:

> She said that Lily was expecting a man named Fred Crabtree to come and stay with her that night. I asked who Crabtree was. She said he was an ex-soldier from Beckett Park Hospital who is going to Canada on Saturday, and that Crabtree had been there last Sunday and stayed all night.
>
> (HO144/6012)

Indeed, the state's concern about any potential connection between Fred Crabtree and Lily's murder resulted in him being traced and interviewed:

> He appears to have been able, however, to satisfy the Police that he could not be the man who left his address at Mrs Waterhouse's house and who is the man to whom the prisoner now refers in her 'Life Story' . . . According to the witnesses whose statements were taken he had a complete alibi . . . The only suspicious circumstance was that on the 1st April he had a slight cut just below his eye, but this was accounted for by . . . a bat [which] had hit him in the face [at work].
>
> (HO144/6012)

Nonetheless, despite the considerable amount of evidence indicating a connection between Louie, Lily and Fred Crabtree, the Home Office Permanent Under-Secretary concluded: 'I have today discussed this fully with the Directors + they both agree that prisoner's story of the presence of a man etc now told for the first time is incredible on the evidence + may safely be disregarded'. He further concluded that the details of the Fred Crabtree found in Louie's bag:

> was *another* patient at the Becketts Park Hospital, and that it seems *probable* he either borrowed Frederick Crabtree's name or that he was of the same name. Fred Crabtree the miner, has a sister in Canada . . . I do not *believe* the prisoner's story, that a man was present when she struck the deceased woman with the poker, and that he subsequently strangled her and carried her body upstairs.
>
> (HO144/6012, emphasis added)

Apart from questioning the likelihood of there being two men called Fred Crabtree living within close proximity to each other, who both attended the same hospital, were both ex- or current service-men and both had Canadian connections, it would also seem appropriate to question the Under-Secretary's use of the words 'believe' and 'probable'. In a capital case, it would seem to be of crucial importance to move *beyond* probabilities and beliefs. In this case, it would have meant carrying out a thorough investigation to establish the identity of this man who had been observed by an independent witness going into Lily's house – and whose details were found in Louie's bag upon arrest. However, as Gilligan and Pratt have noted:

> official discourse is . . . very wide ranging in its scope: it can be designed to bring closure to controversial incidents . . . and it can seem little more than

> simple documentation of the work . . . of a particular criminal justice bureaucracy, written by its chief executive. What such discourse does however, is to provide an official, objective truth about crime, criminal justice and punishment which puts a particular stamp on the available beliefs that individuals and social groups have of such matters.
>
> (2004, 2)

This process of 'truth-production' engaged in by state servants was facilitated by Louie's failure to conform to discourses of acceptable femininity. As 'a prostitute of a low class', 'bad character' and 'very dirty habits' with 13 previous convictions and two illegitimate children – one of them in care – she had broken every one of the conventions associated with domesticity, motherhood, respectability and sexuality, and as such, became the target of judicial misogyny. As a doubly deviant woman she was precisely the *type* of woman who could easily be discredited as a witness. Thus, her attempt to produce 'truth' – based on lived experience and memories in the form of her *Life Story* – could be relegated to the very bottom of the hierarchy of knowledge. Svensson has noted:

> The usual way of piling up a criminal's life in the court records, as well as in the newspapers, is to refer to his [*sic*] life as if it simply consisted of his [*sic*] crimes . . . The person is described as the symbol of evil . . . criminals are regarded as ruthlessly calculating individuals deliberately committing their crimes. There is no regard for the fact that most crimes are committed by people under the influence of drugs or alcohol, often frightened and under stress, or that these acts are often badly planned or unpremeditated . . . [by the] socially vulnerable. Since their voice has been taken away from them they cannot really be heard.
>
> (1997, 89)

In Louie's case, this dominant portrayal of the defendant was exacerbated by her failure to comply with any of the discourses which contribute towards acceptable femininity. Meanwhile, 'establishment forces' were located at the top of the hierarchy of knowledge – largely as a result of their ability to forge official truth into something which 'simply fit[ted] the authorities' preconceived ideas of what really happened' (Gilligan and Pratt 2004, 5). This is further supported by examples of Home Office communications such as: 'The excuse of the murder I do not believe and the law must take its course', and 'The prisoner did not give evidence and the circumstantial evidence of her guilt is overwhelming'. Hinting at the doubly deviant nature of Louie's crime, a third state servant responded: 'I agree. It is the sort of crime that men frequently commit but women very rarely' (HO144/6012).

This completes the *de*construction of official truth and the *re*construction of an alternative truth which includes recently excavated subjugated knowledge – that is – Louie's version of the truth. In the final section I employ the third step in the process of excavating subjugated knowledge advocated by Cain – the application of theoretical reflexivity to the first two steps of the excavation process.

Theoretical Implications

This chapter has not sought to claim Louie Calvert's innocence. Indeed, as I have indicated, Louie herself did not make such a claim. Nor has it sought to suggest that Fred Crabtree – the miner interviewed in connection with the case – was implicated in Lily Waterhouse's murder. However, within the context of state servants themselves raising the possibility of the existence of another man of the same name – or alternatively – someone who had stolen Crabtree's identity, and, keeping in mind this was a capital case with a life at stake – this chapter has sought to suggest that the failure to carry out a full investigation into the exact identity and involvement of this man, constitutes a severe lack of adherence to the founding principles of the British criminal justice system, principles such as 'due process, the rule of law and presumption of innocence [which] play a crucial role in maintaining the legitimacy of the state and its ability to deliver justice' (Ballinger 2003, 219). Directly linked to this, it has thus also aimed to challenge law's claim to truth, impartiality and objectivity by uncovering the processes involved in creating subjugating knowledge – processes which usually remain invisible, as indeed do the processes involved in the construction of 'truth' through official discourse. These processes nonetheless confirm Foucault's observation cited above that 'far from preventing knowledge, power produces it'. It also confirms Inglis's point that 'institutions . . . which claim to speak the truth should be treated with wariness and critical reflection' (2003, 3). Only when such processes are challenged – for example by autobiographies, critical scholars or radical organisations – do they become *visible* – only *then* does the possibility arise for the precipitation of a crisis of legitimacy which may lead to the creation of a new terrain on which subjugated knowledge can flourish, and ultimately, to the formation of an 'alternative truth'.

However, as noted in Chapter 2, the 'battle for the truth' (Foucault 1980, 132) is not fought between equals and the power difference between a condemned prisoner and the entire criminal justice apparatus is emphasised in this case by the state's ability to restore equilibrium after what turned out to be a very temporary crisis of legitimacy – by strengthening its own case through official discourse while simultaneously undermining already subjugated knowledge – to the point where Louie could be annihilated altogether. It was able to do so because 'official discourse is . . . the systemisation of modes of argument that proclaim the state's legal and administrative rationality' (Burton and Carlen 1979, 48). Furthermore, Burton and Carlen's observation in relation to state inquiries can be applied to the inquiries carried out by the Home Office after learning about the existence of Louie's *Life Story*:

> The task of inquiries into particular crises is to represent failure as temporary, or no failure at all, and to re-establish the image of administrative and legal coherence and rationality. One of the political desiderata of official discourse is therefore to retain the intellectual confidence of parties, elites and functionaries within the state apparatuses. To create a discourse of unity and cohesion between parties . . . [thus] demonstrating the state's sovereign reason.
>
> (1979, 48)

The state's success in achieving this goal can be measured by the fact that 'the production of "truth" in official discourse . . . [is] something that had come to be largely taken for granted', as indicated by its ability 'to deny or nullify alternative truth accounts' (Pratt and Gilligan 2004, 9). Within the context of this 'unequalled ability to marshal the available judicial resources . . . and to use them effectively to win their case' (Inglis 2003, 178), an attempt to launch a battle 'on behalf of the truth' is unlikely to be successful; instead the purpose of excavating subjugated knowledge can be understood 'as a battle about the status of truth and the economic and political role it plays' (Foucault 1980, 132). Foucault argues that the intellectual can challenge 'the ensemble of rules according to which the true and the false are separated [as well as the] specific effects of power attached to the true':

> The essential political problem for the intellectual is not to criticise the ideological contents supposedly linked to science, or to ensure that his own scientific practice is accompanied by a correct ideology, but that of ascertaining the possibility of constituting a new politics of truth. The problem is not changing people's consciousnesses – or what's in their heads – but the political, economic, institutional regime of the production of truth.
>
> (in Gordon 1980, 132, 133)

Foucault's position is relevant to the central epistemological point outlined above, which argued against generating another 'true' story or 'objective' body of knowledge (since this will inevitably create a new body of subjugated knowledge), but argued *for* a challenge to 'fake' stories. That is to say, feminist epistemology as applied in this chapter has not attempted to prove that Louie's *Life Story* was more 'true' than the Home Office's version of the 'truth'. Instead, this chapter has provided a systematic challenge to the key 'fake' story that 'truth corresponds with reality and exists independently of people – facts speak for themselves' (Inglis 2003, 172), and that law has access to scientific methods guaranteeing they will be discovered. Far from possessing the scientific means which guarantees the production of an 'objective truth', the chapter has demonstrated the state's involvement in its own of brand of knowledge production and truth manipulation – emphasising those aspects of the case which strengthened legitimacy of Louie's execution whilst simultaneously dismissing those aspects that had the potential to render the execution unsafe.

As noted in the previous chapter, within a hierarchy of credibility where official discourse crowns the pyramid and prisoners 'have the credibility of elves' (Chevigny in Davis 2001, 430), another hierarchy was also evident – that of gender. This gender hierarchy consisted of a 'male judiciary with male definitions and understandings of human behaviour . . . claimed as universal', which, furthermore, allowed knowledge claims to be made 'without any reliance on supporting evidence, empirical or evidentiary' as noted by Donovan in Chapter 2 (1993, 428). This gender hierarchy was reinforced by Louie's failure to conform to acceptable standards of femininity, confirming Smart's point discussed earlier, that 'law is not a free-floating entity, it is grounded in patriarchy, as well as in class and ethnic divisions' (1989, 86, 88), and therefore has a vested interest in reproducing 'the most secure foundations of patriarchal relations . . . the family and gender divisions' (Smart 1995, 129). As a prostitute with 13 previous convictions and 'very dirty habits', the mother of two illegitimate children, one of them in care, and leaving her husband to spend time drinking with other men, Louie had made little effort towards contributing to the foundations of heteropatriarchal family life. Thus, her lack of conformity to appropriate feminine standards stood as a direct challenge to the heteropatriarchal social order as can be observed from the numerous derogatory comments made about her personality, lifestyle and demeanour, quoted earlier. This case-study therefore exemplifies the process identified by Inglis above, whereby state representatives ignored 'the personal . . . meaning and logic of what happened and instead construct[ed] a logic and understanding of events which [were] supplanted by the force of law' (Inglis 2003, 16). This process also constructed the masculinist official discourses that ultimately led to the creation of subjugated knowledge, with Louie's words being disqualified and eventually silenced altogether.

Conclusion

Brown and Clare observed that 'given the susceptibility of the recording of memory to selectivity and interpretation, relying on prisoner accounts will always be vulnerable to criticism and accusation of bias' (2005, 68). In this chapter I have sought to demonstrate that the exact same observation can be made with regard to relying on official discourse. However, as a result of its position at the top of the hierarchy of knowledge, scrutinising its selectivity, interpretation and bias is fraught with difficulties, for, as noted by Inglis above, 'once state representatives have determined what is "true", limits and controls are set on the production of other alternative, resistant truths' (2003, 6). It is within this context that the value of feminist epistemology can be observed, for after having developed the tools for retrieving knowledge from 'below' it has been able to expose official discourse and the legal system – indeed the very foundations of the rule of law – as well as their claim to 'truth' as 'ideological mystifications' and socially constructed products (Box 1983, 13). The fact that the 'symbolic domination of juridical professionals' enables them 'to declare their opinions and theories as if they were facts', and the legal process has named its tools for knowledge production 'due process' and 'rule of law' does not guarantee that conclusions drawn are 'neutral and universally true' (Inglis 2003, 178). Instead they demonstrate that 'truth is linked in a circular relation with systems of power which produce and sustain it, and to effects of power which induces and which extend it'. Hence:

> It is not a matter of emancipating truth from every system of power (which would be a chimera, for truth is already power) but of detaching the power of truth from the forms of hegemony, social, economic and cultural, within which it operates at the present time.
>
> (Foucault in Gordon 1980, 133)

The previous chapter argued for putting 'women's words on paper' and 'giving their words space alongside the author'. It is therefore appropriate to conclude with Louie's words. Before starting to write her *Life Story* she wrote in her exercise book:

> There is so much good in the worst of us,
>
> There is so much bad in the best of us,
>
> That it ill becomes any of us,
>
> To find fault with the rest of us.
>
> (Calvert 1926)

It was not a sentiment she herself was to benefit from, however, by applying the tools of feminist epistemology to her autobiography, it has been possible to bring an end to her muted state and thus make her words visible. In that sense, Louie's *Life Story* has played a crucial part, not only in extending 'a historical knowledge of resistance and struggle' (Sawicki 1991, 57), but also in 'the creation of new discourses and hence, new spaces on which state-defined truth and its claim to value-freedom can be challenged' (Ballinger 2003, 238). As such, both Louie and her story are entitled to be heard and, furthermore, to be restored to their rightful place in history as testaments to the officially sanctioned violence that lurks behind the claim by state servants that their version of law and order is fair, reasonable and just.

4 Infanticide and Child Murder

The 'Leniency versus Harshness' Debate Re-Visited

Introduction: The History of Infanticide and Child Murder

> Much of the current interest in infanticide doubtless responds to the feeling that the last great battle of feminism is being fought over the control of women's bodies. At one political extreme, abortion is seen as the modern version of infanticide, on the other, as the final step to woman's emancipation from biological and legal bondage.
>
> (Wessling 1994, 117)

Wessling's observation above with regard to the diversity of meanings attributed to modern infanticide offers an eloquent illustration of how different 'truths' about a specific event are able to co-exist and run parallel with each other. At another level, the history of infanticide provides a poignant example of the changing nature of 'truth' as different arms of knowledge-producing agencies were able to construct dominant and, at times, competing discourses around the subject. Thus, while the previous chapter illustrated the way subjugated knowledge can challenge official discourse, this chapter is primarily concerned with different aspects of official discourse competing with each other, for, in an era where defendants giving evidence on their own behalf was a relatively new concept, infanticidal mothers were granted limited space on which to construct their own version of events. Instead the majority relied on defending counsel to present their case through existing dominant discourses. Thus, the trials of infanticidal mothers provide further examples of Smart's argument outlined in Chapter 2, of everyday experiences being translated into legal relevances, a process which excludes many points 'relevant to parties', and limits how parties 'are to speak', since their experience has to be 'turned into something the law can digest and process'. In order to provide context for the analysis of individual cases of infanticide and child murder I shall briefly outline the history of this subject prior to the twentieth century.

Jackson has traced the unpopularity and shame of unmarried motherhood to Elizabethan and Jacobean times when legislation ensured 'the maintenance of bastards . . . was chargeable to the parish', which, unsurprisingly, led to 'the parents of such bastards' being met with 'hostility and accusations' from ratepayers, in turn, resulting in the attempted concealment of pregnancy and birth (1994, 66). Kilday adds that 'in pre-modern Europe, "Children of unknown fathers" were regarded as "unwanted parasites"' (2013, 53). 'Within this context the act "to prevent the Destroying and Murthering of Bastard Children"' was introduced in 1623 (Jackson 1994, 66). Unlike the established 'practice of placing the burden of proving guilt on the state . . . the unmarried mother of a dead infant' now had to prove her innocence (Smart 1992, 16). Failure to do so could result in execution. Yet, as observed by Ward, 'excessive punishments led to acquittals of the guilty' (2002, 258), and the harshness of this act gradually made it unworkable, as juries increasingly refused to return a guilty verdict, and it was repealed in 1803.[1] In its place, a new offence was created – the concealment of birth – which carried a two-year prison sentence (Smart 1992, 16). Women charged with this offence were inevitably single and had attempted to conceal their pregnancy in order to preserve their reputation, and who consequently gave birth alone (Jackson 2002, 2). The all-important issue therefore became whether the infant had been stillborn or alive at birth, and as such, a new space was created within the court-room in which to present 'expert' knowledge.

The nineteenth century witnessed not only a vast increase in the collection, and hence availability, of statistics, it also saw a massive development of medical knowledge take place. In turn, these developments had a fundamental impact on the gendered nature of knowledge, as the traditional female professions of midwifery and healing became marginalised in favour of a body of new male professionals, such as coroners, 'surgeons, man-midwives and apothecaries' (Jackson 1994, 68), who 'cast themselves in the role of moral intrepreneurs' (Smart 1992, 17). By drawing on new 'scientific' discourses related to medicine and social statistics, they were able to translate 'a variety of infant deaths into infant murder', which had the effect of redefining infanticide 'as a threat to the social order and civilised values' (Smart 1992, 17; Masciola 2002, 62).

The fact that the 1623 Infanticide Act was only applicable to 'Bastard Children' and therefore, also only applicable to unmarried mothers, coupled with the fact that virtually all those charged under the later Concealment Act were single mothers, has led Smart to conclude that legislation relating to infanticide had far less to do with the preservation of infant life 'than the sexual and reproductive behaviour of a woman who had no man to support her' (1992, 17). As such, these acts can be understood as examples of the phallocentric nature of law discussed in previous chapters – if single women were able to keep their children with them, 'the most secure foundations of patriarchal relations . . . the family and gender divisions' (Smart 1995, 129) would be severely undermined. This point is further reinforced by changes to the Poor Law in 1833 and 1844 which 'made it virtually impossible for unsupported mothers to find financial relief' (Smart 1992, 17). In contrast, rendering such women punishable fulfils law's vested interest in reinforcing the reproduction of heteropatriarchal family relations (Ballinger 2009, 30).

1 For details of the various legal changes to Infanticide Law see Ward (2002).

This is not to suggest that the actual punishment imposed upon women found guilty of infanticide or child murder was carried out in accordance with the letter of the law. On the contrary, as will become apparent below, virtually all the women sentenced to death for this crime during the twentieth century were reprieved (Jackson 2002, 4), and many served no more than three years of their life sentence in prison.[2] Individual trial judges demonstrated on occasion immense sympathy and humanity and the vast majority of juries who returned a guilty verdict did so with a recommendation to mercy. Thus, individual human compassion played an important role in securing a reprieve for condemned prisoners. However, the massive gulf between the nature of the punishment issued and the actual sentences served, can also be linked to the structural issue of legitimacy. With regard to the criminal justice system during the eighteenth century, Hay observed that:

> An ideology endures not by being wholly enforced and rigidly defined. Its effectiveness lies . . . in [the fact] that it seems to . . . [the masses] the product of their own minds and their own experiences . . . the law . . . sacrificed punishment when necessary to preserve the belief in justice . . . In doing so . . . [it] made it possible to disguise much of the class interest of the law.
>
> (Hay 1977, 55)

Hay's argument is concerned with maintaining legitimacy for a social order between profoundly unequal social classes. However, it will become apparent throughout the case-studies that in gendering his thesis, it can also be applied to the profoundly unequal gender order evident during the early decades of the twentieth century. That is to say, during this era, law was prepared to sacrifice the full force of *individual* punishment for the greater goal of maintaining legitimacy for the *structure* of the gendered social order. Analysing punishment from within this wider context highlights the inadequacy of the 'leniency versus harshness' debate discussed in Chapter 1, since from this perspective, the automatic reprieve from the death penalty in cases of infanticide was not motivated by mercy alone, but was also the result of more structural considerations.

At a different level, a complex set of contradictions could be observed within the body of expert knowledge applied to the defendant in the course of her imprisonment and trial. Although a large strand of medical knowledge operated to support and reinforce the interests of law, another strand increasingly sought to explain infanticide through the discourses of pathology in terms of conditions such as puerperal mania. As outlined in Chapter 2, a claim to scientificity is also a claim to truth which, in turn, is a claim to deploy power. As such, the testimony of doctors who claimed to possess scientific proof of murder was situated at the top of the hierarchy of credibility. A charge of murder could only be brought if evidence was available that the child had led a separate existence from its mother

2 The last woman to be executed for the murder of her own child was Louise Masset in 1900 (see Ballinger 2000).

prior to death, and various tests were developed during the nineteenth century to establish this fact (Higginbotham 1992, 272). Despite the notorious unreliability of these tests juries and judges nevertheless placed great emphasis on them, thus medical evidence had the potential to contribute substantially towards a guilty verdict. Higginbotham suggests that 'overzealous coroner's courts' may have classified accidental or natural deaths as murder during a period when medical men were eager to demonstrate their 'technical expertise' in order to gain 'wider recognition and professional status' (1992, 263). In that sense the new medical experts could be observed to play an important part in increasing the number of women standing trial for infanticide or child murder.

On the other hand, although 'by the end of the eighteenth century, medical evidence and coroners' inquests were both established as essential components of investigations into the suspected murders of newborn children', some doctors showed great awareness of the potential implications attached to their expert knowledge and refused to provide conclusive evidence during trials (Jackson 1994, 81). At a different level, the rapid development of medicine during this era could also work in women's favour by providing an expanding range of medical defences to the point where 'it was believed that even labour alone could cause such derangement that a woman might feel driven to destroy her newborn' (Knelman 1998, 151).

Thus, like the legal system, expert knowledge – in this case within the field of medicine – carried its own set of inherent contradictions. However, regardless of whether law and medicine were considered supportive of, or punitive towards, female defendants, undeniably, the focus on infanticide intensified during the latter half of the nineteenth century. In turn, this intensification played a key role in constructing it as a widespread problem which could not be ignored. Higginbotham has linked this focus to the competition for office between medical coroners and lawyers (1992, 263). More widely, Smart, argues:

> The last half of the nineteenth century marks a specific moment of struggle over the use of law to regulate the feminine body . . . [resulting in] an intense legal gaze on issues of reproduction, mothering and sexuality.
>
> (1992, 10)

Within this context, certain behaviours such as infanticide were perceived to pose a particular threat to the social order. Ultimately, therefore, whether the law towards, and punishment of, infanticidal mothers was perceived to be harsh or lenient, both were closely connected to the maintenance of the social order. Thus, as infanticide became increasingly associated with moral decline, 'the whole metaphor of women's bodies became one of instability of womb and mind', and the criminal trial 'became a forum for the public expression and consolidation of such constructions of the . . . unruly feminine' (Smart 1992, 17, 13). Moreover, such constructions help to explain the extreme harshness of a law which punished only one parent for this crime, and which periodically insisted on passing the death sentence upon rape and incest victims who had killed their newborn babies, as the case-studies will indicate. They also indicate the threat infanticidal mothers were perceived to pose to the social order in an era where motherhood was increasingly being idealised and re-defined as 'a specific model of caring activity' (Smart 1992, 15).

On the other hand, so-called 'lenient' punishment – what was to become the almost automatic reprieve of infanticidal mothers – was by no means incompatible with the maintenance of the heteropatriarchal social order. Knelman, for example, has observed that as the nineteenth-century criminal justice system became increasingly patriarchal, it also became increasingly lenient towards women who had killed their babies or children (1998, 146). This leniency, however, came at a price, particularly when it was the end result of replacing agentic, rational explanations with pathological excuses for women's actions, because such a strategy neutralised the perceived threat that these women posed to the social order (see for example McDonagh in Wheelwright 2002, 274). It therefore also minimised the opportunity for the development of an alternative truth. In particular, it undermined the structural causes of infanticide and child murder such as gross gender inequality and the wider social and economic circumstances which flowed from that inequality. In the following case-studies of infanticide and child murder I shall demonstrate how these processes operated in relation to the lives, crimes and trials of three defendants.

The Cases

A Home Office document available at the National Archives includes a list of all women found guilty of child murder/infanticide during the first half of the twentieth century (HO144/1749/419784), and documents relating to all these cases have been examined. Space does not permit analysis of every one of these, thus, the three case-studies below have been selected according to two criteria: their typicality and crucially, the inclusion of the defendants' own words, for the purpose of making the knowledge of the powerless visible, as advocated by Comack in Chapter 2.

Although both the law and medical experts made a distinction between infanticide and child murder, I shall argue that this was in many respects a false distinction, largely the result of the rising medical professions' ability to pathologise women's reproductive functions, a process which allowed infanticide to be attributed to conditions such as 'puerpural mania', which could only be applied to women who had recently given birth or were still breastfeeding (Knelman 1998, 151; Ward 1999). However, in the remainder of this chapter I intend to propose an alternative truth, based on the excavation of knowledge from 'below' in the form of the women's own words, whenever available. This version of the 'truth' places emphasis on women as an oppressed group and the social and economic hardship which flowed from that oppression. It will thus become clear that, whether a woman killed her child at birth or several years later, both types of murdering mothers were united by desperate structural circumstances over which they had no control – dire poverty, abandonment by the father of the child and an overall lack of alternatives (Knelman 1998, 24). In that sense this action can be understood as a rational response to insurmountable and immediate problems. For these reasons infanticide and child murder cases can justifiably be analysed together in a contemporary feminist analysis such as this. Historically, however, it will become apparent in the Hannah Wilson case-study below, that the murder of an older infant was regarded with greater 'significance in court proceedings' due to the fact it had established a life of its own as well as relationships with others (Arnot 2002, 150).

The Case of Florence Boxhall

At the age of 24 Florence Boxhall, a single woman and herself illegitimate, was in 1910 found guilty of killing her newborn, illegitimate infant. She had given birth alone during the night, after which she strangled the baby, put it into 'a sack and threw it over the wall at the back of her lodgings . . . Prisoner went to work next day at the laundry where she was employed + she was arrested there' (HO144/3148). She confessed immediately with the words: 'Yes that is quite right sir. I don't know what made me do it. I had it in the WC.' Having given birth alone and gone to work shortly afterwards, the arresting officer unsurprising reported that 'she seemed weak' (HO144/3148).

Even at the inquest, and thus prior to the trial, members of the coroner's jury demonstrated resistance to official discourse around infanticide by dissenting when the Coroner asked if they had reached the verdict that Florence 'wilfully and of malice aforethought murdered her child':

> The foreman said that one juror thought the verdict should be one of manslaughter. The Juryman . . . observed that he did not see where the 'malice aforethought' came in. They did not know what the conditions of the girl's mind was with their verdict . . . Another juryman expressed the opinion that the man who was equally responsible should be dealt with in the same manner as the girl.
>
> (HO14/3148)

Thus, in the absence of the defendant's own voice some juries attempted to construct an alternative truth on her behalf, and while the coroner responded that 'they had nothing to do with that', he too articulated an ambivalent attitude towards the law and appeared to be caught between the burden of legal duty and sympathy for the defendant:

> He wished the law were altered so that this kind of crime might be dealt with in a way that would commend itself to all people. Of course, the law did not do that at present. This was a case exactly like that of Daisy Lord, and he was reminded that the people who wrote in the newspapers had made a martyr of Daisy Lord, and it was no wonder to him if other people committed such crimes. However, they must not prejudice the case against this girl.

> They were all sorry for her, but that must not prevent them [from] doing their duty. He considered their duty was to find a verdict of 'wilful murder'.
> (HO144/3148)

Thus, while the jury displayed a marked reluctance to impose agency and rationality onto Florence's deed, the coroner did not accept such ambivalence and her trial commenced in November 1910. Even without her confession, securing a conviction would appear to have been almost a foregone conclusion, for the surgeon who conducted the post-mortem left no doubt that he was examining a murder victim: 'The child had certainly lived and breathed freely . . . Death was caused by strangulation + the tying of the cord tightly round the neck' (HO144/3148). Further expert testimony played a key role in confirming this was a case of infanticide. For example, 'the lungs had been fully inflated'. Yet, while neither of the two surgeons who conducted the post-mortem could accept the injuries to the baby might have been accidental, they nevertheless conceded that 'pain + anguish of child birth sometimes makes a woman lose consciousness' (HO144/3148), thereby demonstrating the sometimes ambivalent nature of expert knowledge – and within it – the complex relationship between rationality and pathology discussed above. Nonetheless, Florence was found guilty, 'with a strong recommendation to mercy' (*Surrey Advertiser and County Times* 3 December 1910). Passing the death sentence, the judge commented:

> The jury have returned . . . the only verdict everyone in the Court expected them to come to. No one who has heard the evidence could have doubted that you did, in the desire to hide your shame, take the life of that newly-born child. It is a very, very sad story indeed . . . and I have but one duty to perform. It is a painful one – it always must be, but it is especially so under the present circumstances – and it is to pass upon you the sentence of the law.
> (*Surrey Advertiser and County Times* 3 December 1910)

Florence had not given evidence on her own behalf and the document relating to her case contains only few of her own words. However, her case illustrates the strong feelings of popular resistance to a legal system which, a decade into the twentieth century, continued to issue the death sentence in these circumstances, and where the only route to lesser punishment lay through pathology by denying both agency and rationality. This resistance continued after her conviction through a host of letters received by the Home Office which – in various ways – all expressed disagreement with the nature of her punishment. For example, the growing impact of expert knowledge is evident in Florence's mother's petition for her daughter's life where she attempted to challenge the death sentence by speaking through the 'mad' discourse:

> I implore your Lordship to grant a respite to her, as I firmly believe my Daughter was not right in her mind as she was in Croydon Infirmary for 6 Weeks suffering from Varicose Veins and just after coming out of hospital,

> at times she seemed lost and her mind seemed a blank. Sir, I may state that my Brother has been in Bexley Heath Asylum 13 years for loss of memory and I firmly believe my Daughter lost her mind at the time the deed was done and that she lost all control of herself and did not know what she was doing, she was always a good kind and loving Girl at home and I pray to you Honourable Sir that you will look into her case for me a Broken hearted Mother.
>
> (Letter in HO144/3148)

Other sympathetic observers of the case questioned the legitimacy of her punishment through the 'more sinned against than sinning' discourse, thus, like the jury member quoted above, raising the discourse of masculinity and male behaviour. The letter below is particularly interesting through its author's attempt to increase her credibility by distancing herself from the suffragette movement:

> I am not a suffragette. Therefore I ask you to give my letter your consideration. I am writing with respect to the pr FB now lying under sentence of death for the murder of her baby. I ask you to consider the fact of this most unfortunate case; had it not been for some person doubtless calling himself a man, this poor child for indeed she is little more would not at this moment be in her . . . position. The law we know cannot kick him but it can at least have some mercy on this victim. I therefore ask you to endeavour to . . . grant her a respite, if it is not possible . . . give her an even less sentence. Trusting you will give this case your careful consideration.
>
> (Letter in HO144/3148)

A male sympathiser also utilised this discourse, thus emphasising an argument made in Chapter 2 – that far from being monolithic, masculinity 'embodies multiple dimensions':

> I take this opportunity of writing you . . . with reference to a woman young in life and who's prospects ruined by some Scroundrel of our own sex . . . I think . . . Florence Boxall . . . should be entitled to our fullest consideration with reference to a respite of the sentence passed[,] further that the Poor Creature may be released altogether[.] my name may be added (to any Petition that may be sent to you) upon the unfortunate Woman's behalf and I earnestly Pray Almighty God that you will be able at some future date Draught [*sic*] some measure whereby justice shall be done to both Parties concerned with the child's birth and not the woman bear the blame alone.
>
> (Letter in HO144/3148)

The theme of respectable masculinity evident in this letter was echoed by the local vicar who also pleaded for the early release of Florence and observed that 'the author of this girl's disgrace escaped' (Letter in HO144/3148). Only three days after her conviction Home Office personnel issued a conditional pardon, stating: 'According to the usual practice the case is not one in which the capital sentence should be carried out' (HO144/3148). Arguably, such 'practice' suggests state servants were not indifferent to public sentiment in cases such as Florence's.

Thus, despite Florence lack of opportunity to account for her actions in her own words, a number of individuals, including men from a considerably higher social class than Florence herself, did not hesitate to challenge official discourse and the legitimacy of the law, thereby exercising the power at their disposal to tell an alternative truth about the meaning and nature of infanticide. In particular, they did not hesitate to voice their disapproval of 'scroundrels' who failed to take responsibility for what should have been their marital conduct and breadwinning capacities, as discussed in Chapter 2. Undoubtedly, such opposition to the sentence of death played a role in ensuring the reprieve of women like Florence Boxall – and hence, paradoxically, the restoration of the legitimacy of the law. In particular, the insistence on male as well as female responsibility in relation to reproduction indicates the existence of multiple masculinities within the broader changes in family structure discussed in Chapter 2. Increasingly, men who failed to comply with their designated role as 'benevolent heads of families' could be understood as challenging the heteropatriarchal social order, just as infanticidal mothers had done for centuries, and as such their behaviour was unacceptable to the definers of respectable masculinity (Ballinger 2007, 477).

Florence was released from prison in 1914 to a St John Baptist home where she spent another three years, an unusually long time, recommended and supported by criminal justice personnel on the grounds that she was 'a woman of low mentality' and 'though not weakminded in the medical sense is of weak character and poor intelligence' (HO144/3148).

The Case of Hannah Wilson

As the case-studies unfold, it will become apparent that certain factors were common to the majority of the defendants. Such factors included being classified by criminal justice personnel as 'weakminded', of 'low intelligence', low character' or a 'low type', as the case of Florence Boxhall has already demonstrated. During this period 19 per cent of female inmates in workhouses 'were mothers with children', half of these children's fathers were unknown (Spensky 1992, 104). This undoubtedly contributed towards their stigmatisation as being of 'low character'. Another explanation for being considered to be of a 'low' or 'immoral' type may have been the large number of infanticidal mothers who were deemed to be 'fond of the company of soldiers'. Yet, not all women who 'frequented the company of soldiers' were disrespectable or of a 'low type' (see for example the case of Alice Barber PCOM 8/231). Like Louie Calvert discussed in the previous chapter, several of these defendants maintained that they had discovered themselves to be pregnant after their partners had left for the front. Many such fathers-to-be were subsequently killed during the First World War. In such circumstances single pregnant women were almost certain to be dismissed from their position and with no means of support – financial or otherwise – 'they simply could not keep themselves and their infants alive'

(Smart 1992, 17; Jackson 2002; Arnot 2000). This equally applied to the large proportion of defendants employed in domestic service whose pregnancy was the result of wanted or unwanted relations with other male servants or indeed masters, and who were subsequently dismissed (Kilday 2013, 39; Jackson 2002, 8). Given such severe 'penalties consequent upon unmarried motherhood' infanticide can be considered a rational, if unavoidable, act (Smart 1992, 24). In Knelman's words: 'Unmarried mothers who killed their babies were not necessarily selfish or unfeeling, merely practical' (1998, 154). Such cases therefore also demonstrate the complexity of agency – the women were rational agents, but their actions took place within a wider set of circumstances which were utterly beyond their control.

Cases of child murder followed a very similar pattern, except in these cases mothers had managed to keep their children alive for more than one year, usually by sending the children out to 'nurse' for payment, or by relying on the support of relatives. When such support was withdrawn, single mothers of older children would be in the same position as mothers who committed infanticide – unable to support themselves or their child. Thus, far from these women being 'disreputable', such cases illustrate the hidden victims of warfare, not only in terms of the dead children, but also in terms of turning hitherto respectable and hardworking young women into condemned prisoners, as they alone had to pay the price demanded by a phallocentric legal system which insisted that only the female body was disruptive and unruly and, hence, in need of strict discipline, regulation and restraint (Smart 1992, 7).

Hannah Wilson fell into these categories when she confessed to having killed her 18-month-old child in 1916. After her son was born in 1914, 'by stress of circumstances she was compelled to go with the child' into different workhouses. When she gained employment in 1915, 'her wages were only 11s. 6d. a week, and out of that she had 7s. to pay to Mrs Clark for herself and 3s. for the child' (HO144/1581/323447). Due to the child being 'fretful' and 'delicate', Hannah found it increasingly difficult, and eventually impossible, to find a childminder willing to take him. Moreover, 'the father of the child . . . had been killed at the front. Accused's [*sic*] mother died in 1904, and her father was a drunkard and behaved very badly to his family' (*Evening Mail* 13 November 1916). Within this context she drowned her son. Until that point, Hannah had been regarded as a good mother, and was described by numerous witnesses as having done 'her best for [the] child' as well as being a 'straight and hard working girl' and 'perfectly honest at her work'. The arresting officer, Sgt Howard, further described Hannah 'as a very respectable and industrious young woman' and her most recent landlady testified that she was 'a good sort of girl' (Judge's Notes HO144/1581). Hannah's own explanation of events leading up to the murder indicates her desperate circumstances and lack of support:

> The child was born . . . two days before the war broke out . . . I then went into Gateshead workhouse . . . when it was about one year and three months old . . . I had to put the child out to nurse. I got work, and paid for it.

> Mrs Mullen . . . had it a week or two, and then got tired of it. One or two other people had a look at it, but when they saw it was so delicate they would not have anything to do with it. I was about out of my head. I did not know what to do with it. I don't know what I did. I took it to the water, put it in a sack, and did away with it.
>
> (cited in *Evening Mail* 13 November 1916)

Attempting to identify the boundary between rationality and pathology, defending counsel Paley Scott argued Hannah's case through both the 'victim' and 'mad' discourses and described the case as 'one of the saddest . . . the jury had ever listened to' (*Durham Chronicle* 17 November 1916):

> Accused had done her best to maintain the child. There came a time when she found the burden too heavy to bear, and she found herself no longer able to fight against that adversity which beset her. That little cord by which the human will controlled the human mind snapped . . . and accused ceased to have proper control over what she was doing. The impulse mastered her, and she did what had brought her to the dock . . . It was one of those tragedies of life that followed on love that had not been sanctified by marriage, and also of one of those tragedies where one was left alone to bear the burden that should be borne by two.
>
> (HO144/1581)

Even the prosecutor, Mr Smith, noted that her life had 'been far from happy':

> She . . . had not received any allowance from the father, and by stress of circumstances she was compelled to go with the child, first into Gateshead Workhouse, and then to Chester-le-Street Workhouse . . . the jury would see her state was one of poverty.
>
> (cited in *Evening Mail* 13 November 1916)

Hannah herself was deeply repentant and said from the dock: 'I am sorry for what I have done' (cited in *Evening Mail* 13 November 1916). Nonetheless, after only ten minutes' deliberation the jury returned a guilty verdict accompanied by a 'strong recommendation to mercy'. Following this verdict the trial judge took a most unusual step by adding his own sympathetic voice to the pleas for mercy: 'I beg respectfully to say that in my opinion this is a perfect case for the exercise of His Majesty's clemency' (HO144/1581 Judge's Notes).

Subsequently, Hannah's death sentence was reduced to imprisonment for life, yet, expressions of sympathy for her circumstances continued. The trial judge, Justice Low, wrote to the Home Secretary, expressing his anxiety that 'Wilson should lie under the crushing burden of the life sentence no longer than necessary' (Letter in HO144/1581). When the Home Secretary responded that Hannah could expect to serve a minimum of three years, Justice Low wrote a second letter:

> I was not aware of any practice with regard to these cases and unless you considered it inevitable I should greatly regret this girl being detained as long as three years. It is true that it was not the ordinary case of infanticide and the child was some nineteen months old but I formed a strong opinion that the girl was entirely thrown off her balance by the father of the child meeting his death at the front and was then unable to cope with the difficulties she met with in rearing the child largely due to her difficulties in getting accommodation owing to the child's fractiousness. . . . I have formed the opinion that about two years detention would meet the ends of public justice and I believe that in conjunction with the prison of Durham I might be able to get her assistance on her discharge.
>
> (Letter in HO144/1581)

Justice Low did not live to see Hannah released, but the level of compassion he had felt for her case became apparent following his death when after serving two years, the prison governor wrote a favourable report to the Home Office regarding Hannah's possible release:

> The late Sir Frederick Low . . . was moved by her pitiable past to take a kindly interest in her. He wrote me, and asked me to tell her, that he desired to remain her friend, & would assist her when she was again at liberty & gave her his address. His opinion was that she had worked hard to maintain her child, even to depriving herself of the elementary food to maintain health of body and mind, and that she was distraught when she committed the act . . . Her conduct is exemplary and I believe she will make good.
>
> (HO144/1581)

This favourable report was supported by the chaplain's report:

> A young woman of fair intelligence, good disposition and fairly strong will. A typical hard-working girl. Under normal circumstances I should think she would be a strong good character but the unfortunate position in which she was placed led to the act of criminal recklessness for which she is suffering. She is not demonstrative but she is genuinely sorry for her sin, and I have confidence that she will do well in future.
>
> (HO144/1581)

While the level of sympathy spanning across the entire spectrum of legal personnel reinforces Connell's point that the social order should not be understood as a unified, overarching, monolithic patriarchy, and that hegemonic masculinity is neither a simplistic nor a conspiratorial concept, Strange's emphasis on the existence of 'multiple masculinities' (see Chapter 2), is also evident in Hannah's case, for not all Home Office personnel shared the compassion and humanity expressed by the trial judge, prison governor and chaplain. Instead, they appeared determined to support the staunch phallocentric nature of law:

> Women convicted of the murder of this kind know perfectly well that they will not be hanged and I imagine they very soon get to know at Aylesbury that they will not . . . serve a life sentence or anything like it. Probably they know HO scale of punishment in these cases about as well as we do. Not long ago we had a . . . representation from one of the Lady Visitors as to the danger of treating these offences too lightly: 'Killing the kid' was apt to be regarded as a fairly easy way out of the difficulty. I think 2 yrs detention is too short in the case of a child 19 months old. She should serve at least 3 before going to a home.
>
> (HO144/1581)

This more cynical attitude articulated by Home Office staff thus indicates competing discourses within the state itself about the meaning of infanticide and child-killing, and Hannah served another year in prison after which she wrote a petition which offers the opportunity to 'put women's words on paper', as advocated by Comack in Chapter 2:

> I am petitioning on . . . behalf of myself of having drowning my child . . . in time of madness, worry, despair, not [k]nowing w[h]ere to go or torn from a home had no one to put thing to me . . . I was [illegible] from door to door workhouse to workhouse the nearest workhouse to where I lived second time I went for ticket the head man of the board room of Gateshead told me I had not to go back there any more as he had plenty to do to keep their own people without mine I had not to go, I could not get anyone to nurse him in anyway till my day work was done not for love nor money this lasted for year and half things were dearer his keep and my board were getting higher. I could not follow my work for worry of my child. I got very weak could not eat, when I went home trouble was staring in my face, the night of the dreadful deed God forgive me for what I did as I was not myself, I am very sorry for what I did I had no money to tramp trouble of this [illegible] people did not help me, as my child was delicate and weak it took great deal of money to support him, would you consider my case for me, had no reports punishment [*sic*] as praying to God our maker to forgive me for my first act would you kindly oblige thank you. I wish to ask you could or would you kindly do anything for me in any way. Thanking you, H.W.
>
> (HO144/1581)

Hannah thus attempted to provide a socio-economic context for her crime and in doing so, her lack of support and alternatives became explicit. Her petition was accompanied by a new set of highly favourable reports, first from the chaplain:

> This woman is simple, frank and straight forward in manner, and quiet and gentle in disposition. She is responsive and amendable, and gives no trouble. I believe her to be truly penitent.
>
> (HO144/1581)

Second, from the governor:

> I have always felt sorry for the girl, believing she was more sinned against than sinning. Her conduct in Prison has been exemplary, and she has a Brother + a Sister who will help her if needed: which is unlikely, as she is very competent at all kinds of domestic work. I recommend her in confidence, for clemency. (HO144/1581)

Certain Home Office employees however, demonstrated a breathtaking lack of understanding or awareness of the difficulties involved in surviving in circumstances such as those of Hannah's, reducing the socio-economic factors responsible for her desperation to a mere 'encumbrance', in their consideration of her release:

> This would be rather a lenient treatment of a woman of 25 who killed her baby – 18 months old – because she found it an encumbrance to her. What does the Govn – mean by saying she was 'more sinned against than sinning?' The case is not so pitiful as many infanticides. However if the Govn. & Chaplain's estimate of her character is right no harm would be done by releasing her as soon as suitable arrangements of her future have been made. (HO144/1581)

Thus, in contrast to the prosecution, the defence, the trial judge – and subsequently – the prison governor and the chaplain, Home Office personnel stood alone in attempting to argue Hannah's case through the 'bad' discourse – particularly that of the 'bad' mother – 'selfish, cold, neglectful, uncaring and sexually active' (Morris and Wilczynski 1993, 199) – all characteristics which rendered her more punishable (Worrall 2002). The marginalisation of Hannah's economic and social circumstances in this account of her crime both denied yet reinforced gender inequality in relation to parenthood, paying no attention to the lack of options available to single mothers attempting to support their children. As such it served to support and maintain individual women's subordination within the heteropatriarchal social order. Moreover, this interpretation of Hannah's crime demonstrates the difficulties involved in judging women who kill 'through discourses which recognise their agency without necessarily leading to harsher punishment' (Ballinger 2005, 80).

On the other hand, those who argued her case through the victim/mad discourse also played their part in supporting the social order – albeit unwittingly – for pleading for leniency and emphasising the victimhood or pathology of *individual* women who were no longer able to cope with the level of structural inequality generated by heteropatriarchy, meant that such inequality remained unaddressed. In short, regardless of whether criminal justice personnel displayed a harsh or lenient attitude towards particular individuals found guilty of this crime – the final outcome was ultimately supportive of the existing heteropatriarchal social order. Indeed, the sympathy and compassion displayed by various state servants can be understood as having *increased* legitimacy for an otherwise overly harsh legal system in its policing of a social order, whose structure relied on a profound gender inequality. Ultimately, however, the various pleas for a reduced sentence were ignored as Home Office personnel insisted that Hannah serve the average sentence of three years. In that sense, her case demonstrates both the multi-faceted nature of hegemonic masculinity which allows contradictory discourses to develop within the state apparatus, as well as the reassertion of dominant discourses from within that apparatus as the hegemonic struggle to maintain a masculinist social order continued.

The Case of Ada Cook

Like Hannah Wilson and several others,[3] Ada Cook, standing trial in 1918, fell into the category of a single mother who – against all odds – had managed to support her son for three years and killed him only when she had no means of keeping him alive. Within the context of Ada standing trial for a capital offence the sheer brevity of the case demonstrates the expediency with which justice could be dispensed. The trial transcript amounts to only 13 pages, and the jury reached a guilty verdict after 12 minutes '*without leaving the box*' (Trial transcript HO144/4526, emphasis added). Indeed, Ada's counsel called 'no evidence' for the defence and cross-examined only two witnesses, leading the trial judge to comment in his summing up, 'that Mr McKenna . . . has conducted his case with remarkable judgment and brevity. He has not wasted your time by asking a single superfluous question' (Trial transcript HO144/4526). A more critical interpretation of such 'brevity' may have questioned whether due process and the rule of law were challenged or compromised by the principles of a defending counsel who failed to produce *any* evidence for the defence in a capital case.

As in Hannah's case a year earlier, two competing 'truths' about Ada fought for dominance. The Home Secretary had already stated his criteria in determining the length of sentences in his response to petitioners on Hannah's behalf: 'The actual time which a prisoner is required to serve depends to a large extent upon her conduct in prison, the reports received as to her disposition and character, and her prospects upon discharge' (HO144/1581). Like Hannah, Ada's conduct and prospects were regarded as good by both the prison governor and chaplain:

> The prisoner seems to have a quiet, inoffensive disposition. She has behaved well since she has been here . . . With regard to her prospects on discharge . . . there should be no difficulty in obtaining employment for her.
>
> (Deputy Governor HO144/4526)

> This girl's disposition is good and I believe that she is pendent and sincere in her intention to do better.
>
> (Chaplain HO144/4526)

3 See for example, the cases of Dora Scot (1918) HO144/3434; ASSI 81/64; PCOM 8/300 and Alice Barber (1916) PCOM 8/231; PCOM 8/5; HO144/11692.

Unlike Hannah, however, Ada's character and family background were flawed, with both official and witness statements indicating that she had paid scant attention to discourses of appropriate femininity as discussed in earlier chapters. According to one police report Ada had 'Been in the habit of staying out very late at night + fond of frequenting the company of soldiers. Character of friends and associates both doubtful. Father lazy + drunken been convicted 33 times for various offences' (PCOM 8/242). Furthermore, at the request of criminal justice personnel a previous employer supplied a report which claimed that Ada was 'of a low type . . . untidy + unclean'. Another past employer added: 'I should say very promiscuous + disreputable of late years. Plenty of men . . . so many men she would not know whose the child was' (PCOM 8/242).

Meanwhile, the Permanent Home Office Secretary noted:

> this is clearly a case for respite, but it was a peculiarly cruel + deliberate murder of its kind . . . there can be no question of early release . . . The p[risone]r does not appear to have been in any particular straits and I think she should serve at least 7 years.
>
> (HO144/4526)

A second Home Office employee agreed:

> It is quite clear that this is a case for respiting the capital sentence . . . It is however a bad case of child murder, and I agree that she should serve a substantial term of p.s. I think 7 years would not be too much.
>
> (HO144/4526)

Thus the refusal to consider the wider socio-economic context for Ada's crime – arguably exacerbated by her failure to adhere to respectable femininity – overrode other key factors such as her good conduct and prospects when it came to determining the length of her sentence. Moreover, she did not give evidence on her own behalf during her trial, and as in Louie Calvert's case, negative inferences were drawn from this by the judge who, in his summing-up commented:

> If this woman gave the child to any woman . . . would not you expect her, when charged with murder to say 'I gave it to Mrs Jones' . . . and we could have had them here to testify to the matter . . . but she prefers to rely upon the skilful speech of her learned Counsel and to ask you to formulate for yourselves some doubt of the matter.
>
> (Trid transcript, HO144/4526, 12)

The possibility that her 'skilful counsel' may have advised Ada against taking the stand due to her lack of knowledge and expertise in presenting herself in such a formal situation is not referred to. Arguably, this demonstrates a marked lack of consideration of the social and educational gulf generated by both class and gender divisions, between high-ranking legal personnel and an uneducated women coming from the lower ranks of the social ladder, as discussed in relation to the Louie Calvert case. Ada's voice did emerge however, through several petitions written during her imprisonment, pleading for early release, and her words provided an alternative truth about this crime which challenged the Home Office claim that there were 'no particular straits':

> I humbly ask you to consider my case, I am only 23 years old and I have ruined my life by my own rash act, I was in good work before my baby was born and when my mother knew of my trouble she took me home, and died when baby was 6 months old, the Father of the child had left the county and so I had no one but an aged Aunt to take my baby while I went to work my earnings were not enough to keep us both and when my Aunt brought the baby to me at my lodgings I did not know what ever to do with him, he was very delicate and constantly crying and needing attention for his weakness . . . my old Aunt did not want us, I had not a friend in the world and it was in desperation I made away with my baby and did not realise what I had done till afterwards . . . Miss Shaw of the Women's Training Colony . . . would have me back again and by her help I would try to be a good woman again.
>
> (HO144/4526)

In an earlier petition Ada had written:

> I [kn]ow in my grief and loneliness I did a very wicked thing but I was so distracted I could not think clearly or I would never have done what I did . . . I would try very hard to live a good life and to make up for the past by working hard for my living.
>
> (HO144/4526)

Once year later she wrote:

> I [kn]ow I have done wrong by the great sin I have committed I must have been mad at the time or I should never have done it . . . I do want to make a fresh start in life and to make amendments for the past, and to do what is right. I am exceedingly sorry for the wrong I have done.
>
> (HO144/4526)

Four petitions are included in Ada's case file. All emphasise her desire to 'live a good and useful life', her remorse and her good prospect upon release – all features which may indicate help and/or advice with the construction of the petitions; their contents therefore cannot automatically be assumed to reflect Ada's own story. However, confirmation that she did indeed suffer 'particular straits' and deserved sympathy and leniency came from other individuals and groups, who, unlike Home Office personnel, had known her prior to her conviction. Thus, Dr Helen Wilson, Chair of 'the Training Colony for Women' where Ada had stayed until her arrest, wrote:

> We earnestly ask you to bring this case specifically + personally before His Majesty, + to advise him, by a particular exercise of his prerogative to save this unfriended young woman both from the death penalty, + from the lingering + dehumanising misery of penal servitude. The course we suggest may be condemned by prejudice + unreasoning tradition, but we venture to think that it is in accordance with the highest justice, + that it will be approved by the conscience of the community.
>
> (HO144/4526)

The warden of the Colony also wrote to the Home Office, pleading for leniency by framing Ada's crime within unspecified medical discourses relating to mental illness. This attempt to minimise her rationality by suggesting possible pathological 'causes' of the act, serves as a further illustration of the limited subject positions available to infanticidal mothers:

> Ada . . . told me the whole history, & I felt then, that though one could not classify her as technically feeble-minded, she had no realisation of the seriousness of her crime. She was perfectly happy & docile with me, but seemed as a person in a dream. From my experience with girls, I should have thought the crime almost inevitable, given the circumstances, in one of her temperament. The aunt's refusal to keep the child, because the payment was not forthcoming & she was getting too old to look after it, then being turned out of her lodgings, because there was no room for the little one . . . the dominant thought with anyone of Ada's stamp would be how to get rid of the child, & that would crowd out every other consideration. As she herself expressed it to me, 'I cannot believe I am the girl who did it, but I know I did'; it seems like a case of dual personality, & she is now quite detached from her crime.
>
> (HO144/4526)

Furthermore, a letter was written by the other inmates of the Training Colony, 'entirely without help or suggestion by any member of Staff', pleading her case:

> We feel that if she only have [*sic*] had someone to care for her and money how different it would all have been . . . we who are here to regain our characters cannot express our thankfulness in having such a chance as this & only wish she too had the same opportunity. We would gladly sacrifice anything if you would only take a lenient view of her case and that she could be amongst us again.
>
> (HO144/4526)

Such pleas on humanitarian grounds were further supported by Ada's father's MP, who – after she had spent five years in prison – asked the Home Secretary to consider her release:

> I think this course would be a humane and wise one, and I have no doubt whatever from the circumstances of the family that they merit sympathetic

> consideration . . . I know that it is the tendency of the Authorities to liberate these unfortunate women, who are as a rule a good deal more sinned against than sinning.
>
> (HO144/4526)

Twelve days later he wrote a second letter:

> Since she was condemned to death . . . the law has been altered [Infanticide Act 1922], and now I question whether her case would be regarded as one of murder in the common acceptance of the term. Even, however, if it were, I do suggest that a life sentence modified to ten years . . . was a most severe sentence . . . I do not treat these crimes lightly, but in this particular instance where the entire punishment, both morally and judicially, was vested on the mother, I feel certain that the fact her father . . . is ready to welcome her home and really needs her help, should be a factor in ensuring that liberation . . . would probably lead to her restoration to society on entirely satisfactory lines. . . . I feel convinced that the Home Office will add to its reputation for humanity by taking this step. Not one word of criticism would be possible, and . . . I am confident that the step would meet with widespread approval.
>
> (HO144/4526)

Through such appeals to the Home Office the limited number of discourses available in which to tell an alternative 'truth' about infanticide became visible. Whether the pleas came from uneducated inmates in a reformatory – many of whom had faced circumstances similar to Ada's – or whether they came from members of powerful elites such as MPs, they pleaded her case through discourses of mercy and humanity. In the warden's case, this was supplemented by discourses of pathology through expert knowledge in relation to mental illness. In some cases the letter writers also attempted to challenge the legitimacy of Ada's punishment through offering alternative perceptions of the concept of justice itself. Thus, the Chief Constable from her local area wrote that 'it has all along been felt that a great deal of sympathy could be extended to this woman, owing to the fact that her home surroundings were bad'. In contrast to the Permanent Home Office Secretary who did not know Ada, but nonetheless claimed there were no 'particular straights' to mitigate her action, the Chief Constable revealed a most serious 'dire strait' in Ada's life that was of special significance to her crime:

> I would . . . draw attention to the fact that at the time of the girl's conviction it was suggested that her own father was the father of her child. This man . . . has many convictions against him for drunkenness, assaults etc. [His] place is most unsuitable for the girl, and it is most undesirable that she be allowed, on her discharge, to return to live there with him.
>
> (HO144/4526)

While none of the available documents relating to Ada's case provide elaboration on this issue of incest, a second police officer wrote in his report that Ada's father was 'looked upon in this Town [*sic*] as a very undesirable character' and her mother had died in the workhouse, suggesting extreme poverty and homelessness. Bearing in mind these reports came from police constables, high status individuals who – in the eyes of the state – were and are, situated at the top of the hierarchy of credibility of knowledge, the state's ability to sustain the official discourse that there were no mitigating circumstances, or 'straits', came under increasing strain. In this case the state's own servants, in the form of two police officers, challenged this official version of the truth. Nonetheless, within the context of a gendered social order, it was Ada's character which was scrutinised while her father's allegedly incestuous behaviour remained un-investigated. As such, her case also provides an example of the 'double standard' against which criminal women are judged as discussed in Chapter 1. In turn, this illustrates the limitations of the dominant constructions of female defendants within official discourse: the 'bad' versus 'mad' or 'tragic victim' – more 'sinned against than sinning' – 'to be pitied rather than punished', who should not be held fully responsible for their crime (Ballinger 1996; 2000; 2005; 2008; Morrissey 2003; Allen 1987). As I have indicated, these subject positions competed to construct the dominant truth about Ada as an impoverished, feeble-minded victim versus the 'promiscuous', 'disreputable', 'low type' with 'untidy' and 'unclean' habits, guilty of a 'deliberate' and 'peculiarly cruel' murder. The knowledge held by the state's own servants that Ada's father may have been guilty of incest, that he may have been the father of his daughter's child, that he was of 'very bad character', and that his home was most 'unsuitable' for Ada to return to, did not give rise to a new subject position within which she could be understood to have acted *rationally*, yet, also within circumstances that ought to exclude the possibility of a concomitant increase in punishment, as argued in Chapter 1.

Meanwhile, the determination of Home Office personnel to judge Ada's crime in strict isolation from its wider context mirrored the position taken in Hannah Wilson's case as documented above. Yet, that very position which holds individuals solely responsible for their crimes, regardless of the circumstances in which they occur, also further reinforces Connell's and Strange's key argument that masculinity should not be regarded as a monolithic, universal force around which all men unite. Indeed, this case has illustrated that state servants themselves may be divided around the core values of either hegemonic masculinity or the social order more generally. It is at this particular juncture that feminist epistemology can intervene by situating the actions of the powerless within a feminist analysis that evades dominant discourse, the aim being to create new discourses and subject positions leading to 'increased justice in sentencing' (Morrissey 2003, 35). At the time of Ada's trial, however, such a terrain had yet to enter discourse, for although she was reprieved, she nonetheless served seven years' imprisonment – an unusually long sentence for a crime where the average punishment was three years. Nor did the reprieve entirely satisfy the warden of the Colony where Ada had resided prior to her crime. Instead she widened her argument until it included a challenge to the very philosophy behind imprisonment:

> Thank you for letting me know the decision in regard to Ada Cook. Penal servitude seems such a death in life, it will take all that poor child's courage to keep her mind sane & wholesome during the long years. I do so long for the day when our prison system will be redemial [*sic*], rather than punitive.
>
> (HO144/4526)

The warden thus played an important part in challenging official discourses with regard to murdering mothers, as well as in the struggle to manufacture new forms of legitimacy which operated contrary to the position that the state sought to maintain, as discussed in Chapter 2.

Conclusion

This chapter has sought to challenge the premise on which leniency versus harshness debates in relation to gender and punishment are situated. The fact that all women who had killed their biological children were reprieved following the execution of Louise Masset in 1900, did not and could not demonstrate 'leniency' in punishment since infanticide itself, both legally and commonsensically, was a gendered crime. Instead, we may question the 'harshness' of punishment for this offence – that it automatically carried the death penalty well into the twentieth century, thereby placing the burden of structural socio-economic shortcomings and inadequacies on the shoulders of the very poorest and most powerless in society: individual women who were denied the necessary means to keep their children alive. Indeed, the voluminous amount of resistance to the outcomes of trials of such women as illustrated above, from both the general public and those who had direct connections to the cases, indicates that this 'harshness' *was* questioned and challenged.

In relating such challenges to the themes of this book, it becomes apparent that knowledge from below was already visible to the public and indeed to sections of the legal community. These resisters were engaged in the process of deconstructing official discourse in relation to capital punishment, and, as illustrated above, in many cases had already generated an alternative truth about women who had killed their biological children.

Second, the fact that a number of legal personnel, including a judge, participated in this construction of an alternative truth demonstrates that law itself is contradictory rather than a monolithic bloc, speaking with one voice. Thus, while 'law's ability to impose its definition of events on everyday life' (Smart 1989, 4) has been a dominant theme throughout this book, the resistance to these women's punishment shown by legal personnel, demonstrates the existence of spaces *inside* as well as outside law, on which to generate knowledge from below.

Third, the fact that a large number of men of high status chose to speak on behalf of the accused women confirms Connell's point that we should not waste time on looking for 'patriarch headquarters' – for neither hegemonic masculinity nor law should be regarded as working purely in the interests of men and against the interest of women. This point is supported by Smart, who, while acknowledging women's subordinate position within a heteropatriarchal social order, nonetheless also warns against re-writing history in conspiratorial terms:

> The construction of women's bodies as unruly and as a continual source of potential disruption to the social order has given rise to more and more sophisticated and flexible mechanisms for imposing restraint and achieving desired docility. Yet, we must be cautious of recreating a conspiracy theory of history or assuming an unwavering chain of developments further to subjugate women.
>
> (Smart 1992, 31)

As argued in Chapter 2, law does not consist of 'a rigid system of male domination or patriarchal conspiracy' (Smart 1995, 130), and there are undoubtedly occasions where both masculinity and law work positively for women (Naffine 1990, 102). Yet, as Franzway *et al.* have noted, much of the state's involvement in sexual politics is organised around efforts 'to construct, impose, and sustain a particular patriarchal family form, and to provide an ideological defence of this form' (1989, 12). Thus, while good intentions and a genuine concern for the fate of infanticidal women, as well as a heartfelt desire to support them in their plight, were beyond doubt and must be acknowledged, it is nevertheless the case that an over-emphasis on their victimhood – 'more sinned against than sinning' – to be pitied rather than punished – played its part in the maintenance of existing stereotypes about female conduct and behaviour – that their actions were unintentional – the result of pathology rather than reason and rationality. Individualising and pathologising child-killing in this way thus left the wider, structural, political, social and economic issues unexplored and the interests being served by such processes remained invisible. In that sense an alternative truth about impoverished mothers who killed their children that portrayed them as being 'at once responsible and agentic, yet [also] vindicated and absolved' was never developed, for to have done so would have involved a recognition of their precarious situation being a direct result of a total lack of societal support (Morrissey 2003, 68, 102).

Finally, reprieving infanticidal mothers demonstrated the 'moral' justness of the law, a feature which secured popular approval and legitimacy for the law. As Ward notes, referring to the philosophy of a contemporary judge, Sir Fitzjames Stephen, 'the function of the criminal law was not merely to deter offenders, but to reinforce public morality', a point that 'made it important to avoid too sharp a conflict with "public sentiment"' (2002, 256–7). Yet, arguably, for that very reason, such reprieves also helped to delay legal changes with respect to this crime. Instead, by maintaining the status quo, the re-production of the gendered subject was also secured, in turn ensuring the maintenance of the gendered social order. The key to understanding these women's punishment is therefore not through the 'leniency versus harshness' debate, but through the state's role in the production and reproduction of the gendered social order.

5 A Muted Voice from the Past

The Appeal of Ruth Ellis, 2003[1]

Introduction

This chapter offers a critical analysis of the Ruth Ellis appeal which took place in 2003, 48 years after her execution. The purpose of the analysis is to uncover continuities and changes in subject positions available to women who have killed over the past five decades. It seeks to arrive at a deeper understanding of how it came to be that a case that caused considerable controversy even in 1955, was nevertheless 'heard' in an almost identical manner half a century later. In other words, why was it that a verdict which had caused extreme unease in many quarters in the middle of the twentieth century was upheld nearly half a century later?

The case, involving the last women to be executed in England and Wales, had been surrounded by controversy since Ruth's trial in 1955, as evidenced within the popular media, true crime writing and academic literature (BBC1 1999; Goodman and Pringle 1974; Hancock 1989; Ballinger 1996; 2000; Rose 1993). The appeal was nonetheless dismissed.

The trial had taken place during a decade where feminist activism was relatively limited, whereas the appeal was heard in an era where women had achieved considerable gains, largely as a result of the activities by second-wave feminism. Yet, while 'women have undoubtedly benefited from greater economic, civil and political freedom' (McNay 2004, 171) since the 1950s, ideological progress – following feminist challenges to the discourses of traditional femininity since this era – is more difficult to identify or measure. For example, as discussed in previous chapters, the courtroom remains a gendered space which frequently functions as a key arena for observing these discourses in operation when female defendants stand trial, thus, they continue to have an impact on the capacity of the legal system to deliver justice for women (Ballinger 2000; Carlen 1988; Worrall 1990). As noted in Chapter 2, this delivery is further compromised through law's symbolic superiority in the production of knowledge and truth (Inglis 2003, 3) due to its claim to be objective, value-free and apolitical (Ballinger 2011, 109).

1 Selected parts of this chapter appear in Ballinger (2012).

This chapter utilises transcripts from the trial and appeal of Ruth Ellis in order to provide a critical analysis of this issue. In particular, it argues that in contrast to the easily identifiable economic, civil and political gains experienced by women during the period between her trial and appeal, female defendants have made rather less discursive progress since the 1950s as demonstrated by the lack of new subject positions available to them within the courtroom in the twenty-first century. Morrissey, for example, maintains that even feminist legal discourses rely on a limited range of subject positions and that these frequently mirror mainstream legal discourses – exemplified in the portrayal of women as lacking in agency (2003, 3).

Furthermore, utilising Thomas Mathiesen's concept of 'silent silencing' (2004, 22) the chapter seeks to explain the apparent discrepancy between formal and discursive/ideological gains for women, by identifying the processes involved in maintaining this limited number of subject positions available to women such as Ruth Ellis who stand trial after having killed their abusers. Thus, following Mathiesen, the chapter will demonstrate how potential new subject positions are 'silently silenced' by 'common sense' and 'taken for granted' discourses deeply embedded within jurisprudence and law which ultimately allow them to 'have a disciplining function far outside the ranks of the legal profession itself' (2004, 17). The chapter argues that this disciplining function played a key role in ensuring the Ellis appeal was heard through similar discourses in 2003 as prevailed at the original trial, regardless of the increase in our understanding of the behaviour of battered women who kill their victimisers, including the creation of discourses such as 'battered women's syndrome' through which such cases can now be heard. Within this context the fact the original verdict was upheld in 2003 was predictable and unsurprising.

Unfinished Business: Contesting and Defending the Original Trial Verdict

Ruth Ellis shot her lover David Blakely on Easter Sunday in 1955. Towards the end of the relationship, David had intensified his use of physical and psychological cruelty towards Ruth, repeatedly leaving her guessing and uncertain about the future 'as he see-sawed from promising her marriage to ignoring her for days, even weeks, during which he would be involved in other sexual relationships' (Ballinger 1996, 13). Psychologically drained from this erratic behaviour to the point where she was taking prescribed medication for her nerves, and physically exhausted from a miscarriage only ten days earlier – as a result of one of David's beatings – she finally shot him in front of several witnesses outside a pub in Hampstead.

The details of the case and trial of Ruth Ellis have been widely publicised throughout the past five decades hence, this chapter will not repeat this well-trodden territory (see for example Ballinger 2000; Goodman and Pringle 1974; Marks and van den Bergh 1990). Instead, the controversial aspect of Ruth's defence of provocation which formed the key ground of the appeal will be the focus here, as will a second controversial aspect of the case, which, ironically, was presented by the Crown in its attempt to strengthen the original verdict – that Ruth had had an accomplice who assisted her in carrying out the murder.

At the trial Ruth had pleaded 'not guilty' due to 'provocation', and indeed, the extensive amount of evidence which supported the violence she had suffered at the hands of David was never contested, not even by the prosecution:

> I accept fully that there is evidence before the jury that this woman was disgracefully treated by the man who died, and I accept my learned friend's proposition that it would tend to lead her into an intensely emotional condition, even as that hypothetical person 'the ordinary reasonable human being'
> (DPP2/2430/23271, 69)

However, as the law stood in 1955, no allowance could be made for a 'cooling off' period between the time of the provocation and the fatal act carried out in response to it (Carline 2005a, 16). Instead, Cecil Havers, the trial judge, ruled that 'the whole doctrine relating to provocation depends on the fact that it causes . . . sudden and temporary loss of self-control' (DPP2/2430/23271, 68). Moreover, the acceptance of the 'heat of the moment' retaliation has traditionally been closely linked to how the 'reasonable man' would act – involving the notion that the retaliation must be in proportion to the provocation, or that 'the reasonable person would have reacted in a similar manner' (Carline 2005b, 217; Lacey 2000, 91). As Ruth had not had contact with David for two days prior to the shooting, Mr Justice Havers ruled 'that the evidence in this case does not support a verdict of manslaughter on the grounds of provocation' (DPP2/2430/23271, 71). Extraordinarily, Mr Melford Stevenson, defending, responded by stating that there would be no closing speech on behalf of the defendant, since he did not wish to invite 'the jury to disregard your Lordship's ruling' (DPP2/2430/23271, 72). This resulted in the summing-up commencing immediately after the prosecution's cross-examination of Ruth which consisted of only one question and ended with a particularly damaging reply:

> Mrs Ellis, when you fired that revolver at close range into the body of David Blakely, what did you intend to do?
>
> It is obvious that when I shot him I intended to kill him.
> (DPP2/2430/2371, 58)

The judge's ruling effectively left the jury with no choice as to the verdict, and she was found guilty after only 14 minutes of deliberation.

The second contentious aspect of the case was raised by Mr Perry on behalf of the Crown during the appeal and related to the claim that Ruth had had an accomplice, Desmond Cussen. While awaiting execution Ruth made this statement:

> I had been drinking Pernod . . . in Desmond Cussen's flat and Desmond had been drinking too. We had been drinking for some time. I had been telling

> Desmond of Blakely's treatment of me. I was in a terribly depressed state. All I remember is that Desmond gave me a loaded gun. Desmond was jealous of Blakely as in fact Blakely was of Desmond. I would say that they hated each other. I was in such a dazed state that I cannot remember what was said. I rushed out as soon as he gave me the gun. He stayed in the flat. I rushed back after a second or two and said: 'Will you drive me to Hampstead?' He did so, and left me at the top of Tanza Road.
>
> (cited in Marks and Van den Bergh 1990, 204–5)

Although these circumstances were reported to the police, only a half-hearted attempt was made to locate Cussen, and he was in fact never traced or interviewed on the matter (Ballinger 2000, 321).

The Appeal Hearing

An appeal was not sought after the trial and Ruth Ellis was executed on 13 July 1955, three weeks after being sentenced to death. However, her family's fight to have the conviction overturned finally resulted in the re-opening of the case in 2003 (*Guardian* 12 September 2003).

The appeal judges stated that the case was not 'about the decision as to whether she should have been executed but . . . whether she should have been convicted of the offence of murder'.[2] Hence:

> The appeal . . . primarily focuses on the ruling of the judge about provocation and the consequent directions to the jury. A further point was taken in [*sic*] the grounds suggesting that, not withstanding that the statutory defence of diminished responsibility had not been created at the date of trial, the court can still conclude that factors that might today have permitted such a defence to succeed, render the conviction in 1955 unsafe.
>
> (*Ellis* v. *R* 2003, 2)

The judges acknowledged that David had beaten Ruth on numerous occasions including one where she was hospitalised, and that ten days prior to the shooting she had suffered a miscarriage after he had 'punched her in the stomach'. They further recognised that despite acting 'kind' and 'devoted' he broke all his promises and abandoned her without explanation. In response, Ruth made numerous attempts to contact David by telephone and in person as 'she remained obsessed by his absence and the unexplained change in his behaviour'. She also observed him 'putting his arm around a young woman [and] by now she was

2 In itself, an interesting comment since if Ellis had been found guilty of a lesser crime – i.e. manslaughter, her punishment could not have been that of execution. While the reasoning behind this comment will remain within the realm of speculation, it suggests that the appeal judges, perhaps inadvertently or subconsciously, had considered the punishment, rather than the verdict, controversial.

persuaded that the deceased might be having an affair with somebody else'. On the evening of the second day of David's absence she was 'very upset and had "a peculiar idea" that she wanted to kill the deceased . . . She said that she had not been able to control the peculiar idea that she had formed' (*Ellis* v. *R* 2003, 3–4).

Finally, the appeal judges acknowledged the evidence of the only other witness apart from Ruth herself, to speak on behalf of the defence – the expert testimony of a psychologist, Mr Whitaker:

> the situation in which she found herself was one that she was likely to think was absolutely intolerable for her. She was convinced that he would return to her despite further unfaithfulness and that when he did so she would be unable to resist taking him back . . . women were far . . . 'more prone to hysterical reactions than men'.
>
> (*Ellis* v. *R* 2003, 5)

Within this context the key argument presented on behalf of the appellant was that:

> on the law as it was at the time of trial, the judge was wrong to withdraw the issue of provocation from the jury. It is contended that applying the law as it was in 1955, there was evidence upon which a jury properly directed could have returned a verdict of manslaughter by provocation.
>
> (*Ellis* v. *R* 2003, 6)

In other words, 'since there was unchallenged evidence that at the time of the killing Mrs Ellis was unable to control the impulse to kill the deceased, the issue of provocation should have been left to the jury' (*Ellis* v. *R* 2003, 7). It was further argued that the conviction for murder should be quashed in order to reflect legal changes which have taken place *since* the trial such as 'a much better psychological understanding of what has come to be known as "slow burn provocation"'. Moreover, according to Mr Mansfield on behalf of the appellant, 'the court is entitled to set aside the conviction' for murder in the light of the Homicide Act 1957 which introduced a statutory defence of diminished responsibility (*Ellis* v. *R* 2003, 8).

In response to these arguments, Mr Perry, on behalf of the Crown, argued that 'the only provocative conduct recognised by the Common Law as sufficient' for reducing an offence from murder to manslaughter 'was some form of violent act by the deceased and the only exception that was recognised was the finding by a man of his wife in the act of committing adultery' (*Ellis* v. *R* 2003, 8). Moreover, 'it is not possible to take the purely statutory defence of diminished responsibility created by . . . the Homicide Act 1957 and apply it as if it had been enacted at the date of the killing or the date of the trial' (*Ellis* v. *R* 2003, 9). In any case, there was no evidence that Ruth had suffered from diminished responsibility and 'no act that could properly be seen as a provocative act in response to which Mrs Ellis had acted'. Instead:

> She had responded in a pre-meditated way to the situation in which she found herself, which may have caused her distress, but it was that situation rather than any act or acts of the deceased which caused the distress. It may have been 'transport of passion' but it was a calm, deliberate, pre-meditated killing. The plea of provocation is inconsistent with planning and here there was evidence of such planning.
>
> (*Ellis* v. *R* 2003, 9)

Lastly, her response to her situation was entirely disproportionate, hence the judge had been 'entitled to conclude that no reasonable jury could have concluded, even on the version of the facts that were most favourable to Mrs Ellis, that her reaction was not one that a reasonable woman would have had' (*Ellis* v. *R* 2003, 9).

The Ruling

Nearly three months after hearing the appeal the three judges ruled that it should be dismissed on the grounds that 'we must apply the substantive law of murder as applicable at the time, disregarding the changes brought about by the Homicide Act 1957' (*Ellis* v. *R* 2003, 9). The verdict could therefore not be ruled unsafe on the grounds of a partial defence of diminished responsibility which did not exist in 1955.

With regard to Mr Justice Havers's dismissal of the defence based on provocation, the appeal judges accepted that the Crown's conduct of the case 'on the basis that there could be no reliance on provocation where the killing was carried out intentionally . . . did not represent a correct interpretation of the Common Law'. However, this misinterpretation had no impact on the outcome of the appeal because 'the question . . . is not whether the Crown's view may have been wrong but whether the judge's ruling was in any way based upon such an approach' (*Ellis* v. *R* 2003, 10). The judges were adamant this had not been the case:

> in no sense was he ruling that, because Mrs Ellis had admitted that the killing was intentional, her guilt must follow . . . that was not the basis upon which he ruled that the issue of provocation was not to be considered by the jury. *It follows that this mistaken view of the law had no impact upon the conviction of Mrs Ellis for murder.*
>
> (*Ellis* v. *R* 2003, 10, emphasis added)

The appeal judges were able to reconcile the 'unchallenged evidence that over a significant period of time, the deceased had subjected Mrs Ellis to violent conduct', including the beating which preceded the miscarriage, with their refusal to accept provocation as a defence by arguing that, if she

> had reacted immediately to one of these violent episodes then there can be little doubt, both on the law as it was at the time of trial and as it is now, that

> there would have been a clear issue of provocation that the judge would have been obliged to leave to the jury.
>
> (*Ellis* v. *R* 2003, 10–11)

Thus, the fact that a ten-day interval had occurred since the latest violent attack further legitimised Havers's rejection of the provocation defence.

Apart from challenging Mr Justice Havers's refusal to accept a defence of provocation, Mr Mansfield had also asked for permission to submit new evidence to support his claim that Ruth has suffered from Battered Woman Syndrome (BWS). The judges refused to hear this evidence on the grounds that this condition was unknown at the time of the trial.

The second controversial aspect of the case was raised by Mr Perry on behalf of the Crown, who sought permission to present new evidence relating to the claim that Desmond Cussen had acted as Ruth's accomplice. This too was refused due to 'significant problems that would have to be overcome before the Crown could rely upon this evidence . . . [hence] we considered that the interests of justice did not require us to embark upon this difficult exercise' (*Ellis* v. *R* 2003, 13). However, if such evidence *had* been heard, it was likely that it would have considerably *strengthened* the case against Ruth, since it could suggest:

> this killing was even more premeditated than it must have seemed at the time of trial . . . it would suggest that this was a case very, very far removed from the sort of case in which the law recognises a sudden and temporary loss of self control.
>
> (*Ellis* v. *R* 2003, 12–13)

Thus, despite nearly half a century of controversy over what has almost universally become regarded as an incompetent and inadequate defence, culminating in a contentious execution, and not withstanding the public outcry at the time of the trial as evidenced in National Archive documents (HO291/235; HO291/236), when the Ellis appeal was finally heard in 2003, it *strengthened* her original conviction by dismissing it on legal grounds and rejecting the possibility that the conduct of the legal actors involved had been questionable. The gulf between what has widely become regarded as a lack of social justice by both scholars and casual observers, and the judiciary's insistence that the outcome of the case was a legitimate representation of justice according to the law, is thus wider than ever. At its starkest, the dismissal of the appeal further *legitimated* the execution of a woman who had endured physical and psychological abuse over a protracted period, to the extent of suffering a miscarriage as a consequence of what was to be the last of those beatings by her partner, and who furthermore, had been poorly served by a defence which was dismissed *before* the trial was over, resulting in the failure to provide a closing speech in a *capital* case.[3]

3 Prior to reaching this point inadequacies in this defence included the failure to call key witnesses such as the psychiatrist Dr Rees who had been treating her in the period leading up to the murder,

Yet, on the other hand, within a culture where Enlightenment reasoning is taken for granted and 'facts speak for themselves' (Inglis 2003, 172), the appeal judges' ruling that 'it is not possible to take the purely statutory defence of diminished responsibility created [in] 1957 and apply it as if it had been enacted at the date of the killing or the date of trial' (*Ellis* v. *R* 2003, 9) appears incontrovertible and self-explanatory – beyond common sense. Nonetheless, when juxtaposed, these two positions emphasise the persistence of the chasm between social and legal justice in the twenty-first century and challenge the nature and extent of the progress achieved towards gender equality within the legal system since the 1950s. This challenge is reinforced by Mr Mansfield's attempt to win the appeal on the grounds of BWS, itself a contentious concept [elaborated below] which – arguably – exemplifies the limitations of the progress towards gender equality in recent decades.

In short, while the case has been resolved from a purely legal perspective, for those in pursuit of social justice, the Ellis case remains a troubling example of the long history of social *in*justice that retaliating women have encountered when standing trial for having killed their abusers. The following section explores some of the key arguments behind this claim in relation to the social construction of knowledge and the gendered nature of law.

Retaliating Women, Knowledge Production and the Gendered Nature of Law

> The idea of judicial neutrality is central to current legal ideology in Britain . . . [Yet] judicial utterances about the characteristics . . . of females fairly jump from the law reports . . . [Indeed] for six decades, from 1869 to 1929, British judges wrestled with the problem of whether or not women could be regarded as 'persons'.
>
> (Sachs 1976, 104)

To claim that law is gendered is to claim that it is 'constructed around a masculine subject and an associated set of masculine characteristics' which reflect male norms and values (Davies 1997, 28). Thus, for example, taken-for-granted legal terms such as 'the reasonable person' are imbued with male values because they are socially constructed according to the characteristics of masculinity. As such, masculine constructions are taken as a given and hence remain unspoken in law. Yet, to make assumptions about the population as a whole based on such constructions is to privilege 'the understanding of the world of the group which has dominated legal and public life: white, middle-class, heterosexual males'. Their 'experiences, perceptions and concerns . . . are defined as normal' despite

or witnesses who could have testified that David Blakely, apart from his violent, erratic and faithless conduct, had also been responsible for Ruth losing her job, her home and her money (Ballinger 2000, 317).

the fact that behaviour, reactions and perspectives are all sites of difference according to gender, 'race, ethnicity, class and sexuality' (Hunter and Mack 1997, 182). Thus, experiences and behaviour which fall outside the parameters of this heteropatriarchal norm are in effect silenced:

> this silencing and exclusion is perpetuated by the adoption of an epistemology which posits the existence of objective knowledge and truth which is universal, transcending time, culture and gender, existing outside the realm of human existence. In this framework, there is one reality, and it applies to us all. This reality however, is constructed by the dominant standpoint, thus maintaining power relations and excluding the reality of divergent perspectives. Hence, the male view of reality becomes universal, and the female reality is excluded, thus perpetuating female subordination.
>
> (Carline 2005a, 24–5)

The consequent hierarchy of knowledge which flows from this male-centred epistemology has particular benefits for the legal system which derives legitimacy from its claim to be based on the principles of reason, rationality, objectivity and neutrality, and hence, possesses the tools needed to uncover the 'truth' (Lacey *et al.* 1990, 152; Smart 1989, 11). As noted in Chapter 4, by naming its tools for knowledge production 'due process' and 'rule of law', the legal process and the 'juridical professionals' within it enjoy a 'symbolic domination' of knowledge production that enables them to crown the pyramid of the hierarchy of credibility (Inglis 2003, 178).

This double exclusion of the female experience due to the gendered nature of law *and* the hierarchy of knowledge has specific consequences for legal responses to domestic violence in general, and for the Ellis case in particular, because it is precisely due to meaning and reality being constructed predominantly from a male-centred perspective that retaliating women have experienced severe difficulty in having a defence of provocation accepted.

The origin of this defence can be traced to the seventeenth century when to the 'judicial mind there was no higher degree of provocation that for a husband to find himself cuckolded. Delivering a fatal blow was regarded as fully morally justified, such was the affront to a man's honour' (Burton 2001, 254). Not until 1946 did the judiciary finally accept that the defence of provocation could also be utilised by wives who had killed their husbands (Taylor in O'Donovan 1991, 226). The provocation defence is thus a powerful example of 'the manner in which law has been constructed from a male perspective, according to male standards, so that it either excludes, devalues or distorts women's experiences and motivations' (Fox 1995, 171). In turn, this helps to explain why male domestic killers have frequently been able to utilise 'provocation' as an excuse for their crime, while women, historically the property of men, have not (O'Donovan 1991, 224; Burton 2001, 254). Instead, due to the gendered nature of law, retaliating women have had to rely on explanations and subsequent defences which confirm stereotypical notions of female characteristics, conduct and behaviour. Thus, while in recent decades the legal system has undeniably made efforts to recognise the specific circumstances in which battered women kill their abusers (Burton 2001, 253; Carline 2005a, 29; Leader-Elliott 1997, 166), the specific manner in which the law has adapted to take account of these circumstances remains highly contentious, with one form of stereotyping replacing another, as exemplified by the widespread adoption of BWS as a partial defence (Nicolson and Sanghwi 1993, 735).

Originally introduced to assist women defendants by demonstrating their 'actions were reasonable given the circumstances', BWS was soon appropriated to reinforce traditional discourses of femininity and is now mainly utilised to support the defence of diminished responsibility (Morrissey 2003, 73; Worrall 2002, 57; Fox 1995, 182). Law's willingness to adopt BWS as a partial defence may thus be linked to the ease with which it could be made to reflect dominant stereotypes of femininity. Carline notes:

> Whilst significant gains may have been made in relation to the growth of manslaughter over murder convictions, and reduced sentences, this advantage has come at a considerable cost of constructing women in a stereotypical and negative manner.
>
> (2005a, 33)

Such stereotyping not only has detrimental consequences for the development of subject positions which can take account of female agency, but also for the inclusion of a wider social context within which violence against women is commonplace:

> the focus on syndromes, psychosis and depressive conditions' so frequently evident in the defences of battered women who have killed their abusers empty the woman's act of external social meaning and act as a 'safety valve' for criminal law's refusal to consider the social context and causes of crime.
>
> (Nicolson 2000, 171)

Thus, legal changes introduced in recent decades which at first glance appear to be progressive developments in dealing with the specific circumstances surrounding retaliating women, on closer examination turn out to 'reinforce notions of female inferiority, passivity and weakness', leading Nicolson to argue that 'what the law giveth, it also taketh away' (2000, 170). It is thus questionable to what extent these developments equals 'progress' for while they have undoubtedly resulted in a measure of success in terms of the outcome of individual trials as evidenced in notorious cases such as those of Thornton, Humphrys and Aluwalia (Nicolson and Sanghvi 1993; Stanko and Scully 1996; Minkes and Vanstone 2006), the discursive battle continues with little indication that new subject positions are about to be legally recognised. As Jackson notes: 'Legal reform, without a fundamental overhaul of the interpretative background, amounts to little more than tinkering with the edges of systematic and structural injustice' (cited in Chan 2001, 169).

Having deconstructed the gendered nature of law and the heteropatriarchal nature of judicial knowledge production as discussed in Chapter 2, feminist analysis is able to identify key issues which were evident in both the Ellis trial and appeal, and remain the focus of feminist debate in the twenty-first century. They include the limited number of subject positions and 'gender constructions available for women who kill' (Carline 2005a, 35); the de-contextualisation of this crime and the phallocentric nature of legal knowledge production, all features which were also evident in the cases analysed in the previous two chapters. In what follows, specific aspects of the Ellis appeal ruling are identified for analysis in order to demonstrate how continuities within judicial epistemology have contributed towards the maintenance of the chasm between legal and social justice over the past half a century, and thus also towards the inability to deliver justice for retaliating women.

Hidden and Silent Continuities in Law since 1955

> [Although] overt discrimination by law on the basis of sex has been more or less eliminated with the attainment by women of full formal status as legal persons . . . it remains the case that many areas of law are gender-specific in that the discriminations which they enforce are gendered.
>
> (Davies 1997, 29)

Prior to its replacement with 'loss of control' defence in 2010, the provocation defence had periodically been re-visited and re-formulated since 1955. Yet a definition of it, guaranteeing legal as well as social justice for both men and women, remained elusive, and the Ellis appeal exemplifies the fact that contentious issues within it remained unresolved into the twenty-first century. The following analysis does not seek to provide a detailed or complete account of the legal changes to provocation since 1955. Nor is it intended to challenge the accuracy of the *legal* outcome of the appeal. Instead, it focuses on the hidden and 'silent' nature of gendered assumptions that remain deeply embedded within the operation of the judiciary, regardless of the expansion of equality legislation, for it is these very assumptions which can be understood as contributing factors towards the chasm between social and legal justice for retaliating women. Davies's words capture the essence of this process:

> The law is seen to be gendered because it takes up abstract gender characteristics in particular ways, while carefully avoiding sexual specificity or overt discrimination on the basis of sex. Using this style of thinking, we could even say that the law prohibits sex discrimination, but entrenches, assumes, and often requires gender discriminations.
>
> (1997, 29)

This process can be observed in action in the Ellis ruling, when the judges considered two major inter-related aspects of the feminist critique of the provocation defence – qualifying trigger events and time lapse. First, they stated that 'a violent response . . . might . . . be considered not to be unreasonable if the whole background was taken into account. This is the whole basis of the concept of "slow burn provocation"' (*Ellis* v. *R* 2003, 11). Thus, they had demonstrated recognition of the gendered nature of retaliation in response to provocation and responded to the feminist demand that 'the context of a history of violence' must be considered (Burton 2001, 253).

Second, they quoted from Lord Hoffman's ruling in *R* v. *Smith* (Morgan) [2001] that 'male possessiveness and jealousy should not today be an acceptable reason for loss of self control leading to homicide' and concluded that 'we can see no proper basis for distinguishing between male and female behaviour in this regard' (*Ellis* v. *R* 2003, 12–13). Here the judges addressed another key feminist critique – the acceptance of provocation based on 'faithless conduct or disenchantment' following murder by men of an erring female spouse (Burton 2003, 280). Their refusal to accept this defence, coupled with their determination to enforce legal equality between the sexes in such cases thus appeared exemplary.

However, in their consideration of the 'triggering event', some form of *action* must occur to qualify as justification for retaliation (*Ellis* v. *R* 2003, 11). In 1955 'the only provocative conduct recognised by the Common Law as sufficient for these purposes was some form of violent act by the deceased' (*Ellis* v. *R* 2003, 13). The judges confirmed the contemporary validity of this definition by reiterating that 'even the modern approach . . . [requires] something more than mere possessiveness and jealousy'.

> There was no event of the requisite kind that could have triggered this killing after the physical violence preceding the miscarriage. This attack had taken place approximately a fortnight before the killing.
>
> (*Ellis* v. *R* 2003, 12)

In short, despite the judges' reference to 'slow burn', this state of mind must still culminate in a qualifying trigger according to the masculine norm (Munro 2007, 134). In the Ellis appeal, the failure to do so resulted in 'slow burn' being re-defined as 'inaction' within a legal definition of provocation where only 'the male model of violent response to behaviour qualified as provocative is ruled in' (O'Donovan 1991, 224). The judges stated:

> Everything alleged is in reality an *omission* rather than a positive act. Mr Mansfield argues that although omissions they nonetheless involved positive acts. For example the failure to go back to Mrs Ellis is an omission seen in that sense but it involved the positive act of going to the Findlaters [*sic*] home. Whilst we recognise the force of this argument what 'provoked' Mrs Ellis was not the going to the Findlaters [*sic*] home but the failure to come back to her.
>
> (*Ellis* v. *R* 2003, 11, emphasis added)

Yet, it was precisely this 'inaction' – this 'omission' – that fuelled Ruth's 'slow burning anger' throughout the weekend which culminated in the killing. Within the wider context of her relationship with David, the longer the omission lasted – the greater she felt provoked, as 'the fires of her jealous insecurity [were being] continuously stoked during the last week before the murder' (Hancock 1989, 185). Moreover, whilst recognising that 'law operates with an extremely narrow conception of those situations in which an omission can take the place of an act', it is nevertheless the case that 'a failure to act is not "just nothing"' and 'omission can be as much the cause of an event as acts' (Norrie 2001, 120; 121). Law's failure to recognise this in both the trial and appeal of the Ellis case confirms the continuity of phallocentric assumptions within it because it could not, and cannot, comprehend that 'inaction' reinforces women's existing powerlessness and lack of control. As such, inaction or 'omissions' are experienced in gender-specific ways and accordingly carry particular meaning, hence, may indeed become part of the 'trigger event' where retaliating women are concerned. Law however, takes a '"wholly unrealistically restrictive view" on provocation' which relates 'not only to the male model of violent response to behaviour qualified as provocative, but also to the limitation of the notion of provocation to certain actions and incidents' (O'Donovan 1991, 224). In short, the gendered nature of the 'trigger event' could not, and, in the twenty-first century, still cannot be articulated or understood within phallocentric law. O'Donovan notes:

> What seems to be overlooked by defence lawyers and judges is the notion of the 'slow burn', that is, the gradual build up in the powerless of feelings of anger and helplessness which eventually erupt, but not necessarily at a moment suitable for the definition of provocation.
>
> (1991, 224–5)

Thus, the lack of a 'recent' trigger and the consequent time lapse in the Ellis case is in fact typical in cases of retaliating women (Burton 2001, 248; O'Donovan 1991; Barnett 1998; Edwards 2010). Yet, the appeal judges ruled:

> It was never suggested by Mrs Ellis that she had acted as a result of this earlier violence and it would, in reality, on the evidence have been quite impossible for her so to do [*sic*]. It is an essential feature of such provocation that there is 'sudden and temporary loss of self control'.
>
> (*Ellis* v. *R* 2003, 12)

This statement affirms the understanding of the law as it stood in 1955, only six years after Lord Devlin had ruled that '"the further removed an incident is from the crime, the less it counts"' (cited in O'Donovan 1991, 223). However, the judges' acceptance of Devlin's ruling in 2003 adds contemporary affirmation to the masculine reaction to violence, associated with an immediate response to provocation as a result of anger, rather than a delayed response as a result of '"a state of despair" that may drive an abused woman to kill' (Burton 2001, 251; Carline 2005a, 25).

In sum, the Ellis appeal ruling serves as an illustrative example of Nicolson's claim that 'what the law giveth, the law taketh away', for despite the appeal judges' *inclusion* of a gendered context and *exclusion* of the sexist 'faithless conduct and disenchantment' defence, their ruling nevertheless confirmed that the experiences of retaliating women still cannot be accommodated; instead, their knowledge about violence remains subordinated within contemporary law (O'Donovan 1993, 430).

The issue of immediacy 'has engaged feminist and legal scholarship' since the 1970s (Edwards 2010, 226) because a delay is constructed as either leading to revenge or calming down, both of which result in a legal construct within which the person is rational and calculating, hence, in possession of 'legal responsibility' (O'Donovan 1991, 228). Consequently, it has repeatedly been addressed since 1955, and to some extent discredited, particularly since the cases of Ahluwalia, Thornton and Humphreys during the 1990s (Minkes and Vanstone 2006; Stanko and Scully 1996; Nicolson and Sanghvi 1993). Yet, it remains a contentious and gendered issue within law as the Ellis appeal illustrates. This was reaffirmed with the introduction of the 'loss of control' defence in 2010, where, despite the removal of the 'immediacy principle' Edwards maintains that 'a lapse of time will nevertheless be taken into consideration as background circumstances', weakening this defence to the point where a jury 'may not concur with her assessment that the killing was justifiable'. This is important because 'a battered woman's reaction to her abuser's violence does not necessarily follow from the severity of the last act of violence'. Conversely, the battered woman may consider 'that she has a justifiable sense of being seriously wronged, but where the last qualifying trigger is not in itself extremely grave' (2010, 226, 233).

Virtually every aspect of Edwards's critique could have been written specifically for the Ellis case, yet, it is written in response to the latest law reform – loss of control – designed to improve the way in which cases like hers are dealt with – such is the power of the continuity of phallocentric discourses within law. This is unsurprising since it is sustained by the very nature of legal reasoning where every norm within the 'system must in some way be validated by a higher reference point which is also within the system' (Davies 2007, 160), thus ensuring a self-perpetuating logic and method of reasoning which can only ever consider issues which are already legally recognised:

> Legal methods for determining truth come from within its own system. The rules and procedures by which the content of law is determined are legal rules. Rules of evidence determine what the knower can know, what the 'relevant facts' are, the story that the object who is known can bring into the court. Where a context over knowledge occurs judicial pronouncements as to truth have high status.
>
> (O'Donovan 1993, 431)

In contrast, the factors by which women's '"difference" is constructed are social' rather than legal in character, and it is this characteristic which excludes them 'from having their subject positions represented by law' (Davies 2007, 161). Thus, the progress in establishing legal equality has had little impact upon creating new *subject* positions for retaliating women since legal changes merely introduce reform to existing subject positions – they do not address women's subordinate position within the social order where the problem of domestic violence itself is rooted:

> Through the reform process law may appropriate new ideas, narratives, or doctrines, but this does not necessarily entail a change to law's basic technologies of exclusion.
>
> (Davies 2007, 162)

In other words, relying on law to remedy problems it itself has created – the disqualification of 'women's accounts and experiences' – allows its power as 'a system of knowledge' with a monopoly on 'the definition of events' (Smart 1989, 86, 162) to remain unchallenged:

> Law's power to name its own boundaries enables it to define a particular question as outside its scope and responsibility . . . the cloak of neutrality hides . . . the power of the judge as knower, and the difficulties for outgroups in bringing their knowledge to legal attention.
>
> (O'Donovan 1993, 432)

This continuity of phallocentric law becomes exposed when considering how *male* subjectivities – through 'patriarchal narratives of provocation have been incorporated into law and recognised by its hierarchy. They are appropriately validated and have the correct "pedigree"', hence:

> The subjectivity of men who react suddenly and aggressively to what they see as provocative conditions has been legally valued over that of their . . . female victims and . . . over the subjectivity of women who have been assaulted for years and who end it by killing their partners.
>
> (Davies 2007, 161)

Davies's analysis has particular significance for cases of separation homicides like Ellis's – a category usually noted for the over-representation of men whose killing is 'motivated by possessiveness or jealousy resulting from the breakdown of a relationship' (Leader-Elliott 1997, 150), because it helps to explain why, in sharp contrast to the Ellis ruling, the departure of a *female* spouse – and her subsequent failure to return to her male partner – is not constructed as 'inaction' or 'omission'. On the contrary, despite departing female spouses belonging to the group 'most likely to be battered or killed', when male perpetrators stand trial for their murder, separation is understood and accepted as the 'trigger event' and can become a mitigating circumstance in itself (Messing and Heeren 2009, 182). Ironically, then, in her pursuit and murder of an erring partner, Ruth had in fact killed according to 'a typical masculine pattern' (Leader-Elliott 1997, 152) – conforming to the role culturally scripted for men. Thus, the fact that neither David's departure nor his unfaithfulness were constructed as 'triggers' leading to the killing during either the trial or appeal goes to the very heart of phallocentric continuity in law, illustrating what is 'understood as "normal" in society' (Norrie 2001, 121) is itself phallocentric. In this case the taken-for-granted assumption that 'sexual provocation . . . claims for itself a constituency almost exclusively masculine', was revealed (Leader-Elliott 1997, 153). In that sense the ruling offers a rare opportunity for the exposure of the continuation of deeply embedded – usually hidden – gendered assumptions inherent within legal proceedings, despite substantial progress in implementing legal and formal equality since 1955. Indeed, the ruling serves as another example of the ongoing process whereby legal proceedings ignore 'the personal . . . meaning and logic of what happened' and instead construct a logic and understanding of events built on masculinist official discourse, re-enforced by legality and law (Inglis 2003, 16) as explained in Chapter 3. Had this process not been ongoing, the failure to identify David's behaviour as the trigger would have been noted for its absence – itself an example of 'omission'. Instead it serves as another reminder that women's 'difference' is constructed within the social arena, and 'the narrow law of omissions excludes the social context in order to draw a tight line around those whose conduct has already been constructed as deviant by the state and its various actors' (Norrie 2001, 121, 133).

Yet, David's departure – together with his various affairs and general womanising, including the fact that Ruth had observed him with 'his arm around a young woman' shortly before the murder – constituted behaviour amounting to more substantial provocation than that which frequently qualifies as trigger events when contemporary male killers claim provocation as part of their defence in similar circumstances:

> There are plenty of examples in the late twentieth [and twenty-first] century of men successfully pleading provocation relying on what their partners *allegedly* said to them. Not even prosecutors question the confessions of adultery, or taunts about sexual prowess which defendants claim provoked them to kill.
>
> (Burton 2001, 254–5, original emphasis; see also Burton 2010, 164; Wardrop 2009)

Once again taken-for-granted assumptions around 'normality' are relevant because it is rare for women to kill a departing partner, particularly an abusive one, as Ruth did, for while 'both men and women are seeking relief from pain induced by separation . . . they do so in a gendered manner' (Messing and Heeren 2009, 284). Ruth however, failed 'to conform to approved "gendered scripts"' which resulted in her subject position becoming that of 'an unintelligible gender' – rendering her version of events silent (Carline 2005b, 216), thus closing down the opportunity for a more complex explanation in both the trial and appeal. Consequently, her anguish went unrecognised as mitigation and the meaning that her act carried for her as an individual could not be understood:

> requirements of criminal law defences produce and perpetuate the silencing of women, especially in relation to domestic violence. This silencing occurs due to the dominance of the male gender . . . [resulting in] the voices and experiences of women [being] ignored. Reality and truth is based upon the male voice and the female voice is excluded.
>
> (Carline 2005a, 24)

The ongoing failure to create new subject positions for retaliating women such as Ellis meant that, as in 1955, her identity in 2003 still carried the threat of a 'crisis of sexual difference' and her femininity could appear only 'as inappropriate and out of place' (Rose 1993, 50–1). In turn, this failure to create new subject positions can be related to the stability and continuity of the actual *operation* of law – particularly the 'ability to impose its definition on events of everyday life' (Smart 1989, 4), as noted in previous chapters. This ability is reinforced by its position at the top of the hierarchy of credibility where knowledge production is concerned, thus, reinforcing Inglis's observation discussed in Chapter 3, that once state representatives who speak through legal discourses 'have determined what is "true", limits and controls are set on the production of other alternative, resistant truths' (Inglis 2003, 6), thereby, further enhancing its operational stability.

In sum, despite the apparent 'progressive' changes to law since the Ellis trial – beginning with the introduction of the 'diminished responsibility' defence in 1957, and culminating in the 'loss of control' defence in 2010 (*Ministry of Justice Circular 2010/13*) – the outcome of the Ellis appeal nevertheless symbolises the *maintenance* of the gendered nature of law in particular and the social order in general. Utilising Mathiesen's concept of 'silent silencing' I now explore some key factors which sustain this resilience to structural changes within the legal system. Implicit to this analysis is the identification of the processes which prevent new subject positions from developing, despite the protracted onslaught of feminist critiques of phallocentric law.

Silence Unplugged

> Jurisprudence contains a peculiar potential to transform political questions of conflict into apparently neutral, technical and professional questions – something which . . . silences the rest of us when confronting the questions.
>
> (Mathiesen 2004, 17)

In his book *Silently Silenced* Mathiesen is concerned with the way in which 'silencing' works 'as an insidious force' to prevent political action from developing (2004, 14). The burgeoning volume of feminist critique represents a sustained challenge to phallocentric law and indicates vigorous political activity. Yet, as demonstrated above, the response to this onslaught of activism has manifested itself in legal *reform* to the *existing* system, rather than the creation of new subject positions. Thus, various reforms since the Ellis case took place unarguably takes feminist critiques into account, yet can also be understood as examples of

Mathiesen's concept of 'absorption'. O'Donovan notes that 'failure to change caries its own risks to legitimacy' (1993, 434), hence, far from being impervious to feminist activism, a number of reforms implemented since the 'diminished responsibility' defence in 1957 testify to law's awareness of, and response to, vociferous feminist critiques. However, instead of responding to the demand for new subject positions, these reforms demonstrate an ability to absorb progressive goals: 'goals are given "rounded edges" so they are not threatening to the prevailing order' (Mathiesen 2004, 15). Thus, instead of retaliating women being 'able to tell their own stories in court', the 'translation of feminine agency and responsibility into masculine understandings of irrationality and provocation' (Morrissey 2003, 102) continues, irrespective of legislative changes: 'attitudes and actions which in origin *are transcendent are integrated in the prevailing order in such a way that dominant interests continue to be served.* This way, they are made unthreatening to the prevailing order' (Mathiesen 2004, 15, original emphasis). In this case, phallocentric law and the heteropatriarchal social order are maintained, for despite legal changes, women's knowledge remains excluded from the courtroom unless mediated by expert knowledge (Ballinger 2003, 228; Worrall 2002, 57; Fox 1995, 182) as exemplified by BWS, which 'shifts attention away from the intolerable conditions in which abused women live' (O'Donovan 1993, 431).

Mathiesens's concept of 'legalisation' is also relevant to the analysis of the operational stability of law, because 'the distinctive form of talk or presentation of lawyers constitutes a language of power which in itself has a strong silencing effect on others'. Mathiesen's emphasis on the power of jurisprudence to determine 'what falls "inside" and what falls "outside" a particular line of reasoning' chimes with the feminist critique of legal reasoning outlined above. He adds that the emphasis on 'legal basis' for given actions transforms 'a clearly political debate – for and against a political standpoint – to being an exchange of opinions concerning the apparently neutral and unpolitical issue of whether legal authority or basis "exists"' (Mathiesen 2004, 17). This process was evident in the Ellis trial, during the gendered (political) construction of what constitutes 'provocation' which was reduced to the 'precedent' (non-political) of the *Holmes* v. *DPP* 1946 ruling (*Ellis* v. *R* 2003, 6). Half a century later, it was still evident in the appeal where the same set of gendered (political) debates was reduced to, apparently, non-political differences between common and statute law. It was further evident when Cussen's involvement in the crime was raised. His role – supplying a loaded gun to an intoxicated, traumatised, distraught woman before transporting her to the scene of the crime – when discussed within a *gendered* context, arguably *reduces* Ruth's culpability (Ballinger 2000; BBC1 1999). However, when transformed into a *legal* issue, it becomes a case of conspiracy to murder, thereby *strengthening* the Crown's case. For Mathiesen this process involves the 'lifting' of the debates 'from the political to the professional-juridical level, the professional-juridical level being regarded as superordinate and therefore more "elevated"' (2004, 17).

It is when this process of legalisation is brought to the forefront of analysis that phallocentric law's ability to deny new subject positions for retaliating women becomes most visible, for within a system of knowledge production built on legal-patriarchal commonsense, it appears 'obvious' that the Ellis appeal could not be heard within the context of a partial defence created *after* her trial (BWS), and that, if she and Cussen had planned the crime together, she had committed the additional crime of conspiracy to murder. The power of commonsensical language 'enables a claim that legal knowledge is not artificially limited', that judges 'are in touch with the everyday world, that they know what ordinary folk think . . . From this evocation of human nature and ordinariness comes a judgement of normalcy and law's claim to universality' (O'Donovan 1993, 433). Thus, the utilisation of common sense disguises law's own epistemological stance – it remains hidden and therefore difficult to challenge. Yet, given the important role that judges play in 'determining what passes for common sense' (Morrissey 2003, 37) it is important to understand and deconstruct these processes, for new subject positions can only be developed after the dismantling of existing, dominant regimes of truth production (Foucault 1980, 132, 133).

The fact that women's knowledge can only be heard via experts while men's 'definitions and understanding of human behaviour' (O'Donovan 1993, 428) can claim universal status – goes a long way to explain the misfit between social and legal justice. The power of legal-patriarchal discourses ensures they themselves can decide which issues can be challenged or discussed. Feminist knowledge – constructed within the social – falls outside the framework of legal reasoning. It is, in Foucauldian terms:

> A whole set of knowledges that are either hidden behind more dominant knowledges but can be revealed by critique or have been explicitly disqualified as inadequate to their task or insufficiently elaborated: naïve knowledges, located low down on the hierarchy, beneath the required level of cognition or scientificity.
>
> (Foucault 1980, 82)

This 'scientificity' also contributes to 'silent silencing' because scientific positivism abound in the phallocentric courtroom where only the '"positive", projecting or protruding knowledge . . . shows itself [and is] registered' (Mathiesen 2004, 25). This helps to explain why, within phallocentric law, David's separation from Ruth became constructed as a 'failure to return' – an *omission* – it did not count as an act either in 1955 or 2003. The taken-for-granted 'scientific' method of constructing 'truth' within legal discourse is indicated by its ability to dismiss alternative truth accounts produced from an experiential viewpoint. Yet, silent silencing is a subtle, non-conspiratorial process:

> The actual silencing of opinions and actions which in fact continually takes place . . . is hidden both to the participants themselves and to the spectators. No external orders . . . or noisy methods are brought in. The surface is clean and shiny, we do not see the political silencing which in fact is there.
>
> (Mathiesen 2004, 24–5)

Nonetheless, the five strategies identified by Mathiesen as necessary to the maintenance of 'hidden silencing' are all represented in the Ellis case and further illuminates how continuities within the trial and appeal have been sustained. The first of these is 'individualisation'. By prioritising the legal over the social, law in 2003 as in 1955 *individualises* cases of retaliating women, thus ensuring inequalities inherent within relationships between men and women remain unchallenged. In turn, this strategy contributes towards the maintenance of the gendered social order.

Mathiesen's second strategy – 'normalisation' – may seem paradoxical to 'individualisation'; however, the two complement each other, for the event must not be individualised to the point where it becomes inexplicable, since concern may then be raised on *that* basis. Thus, the Ellis case was compared to other cases involving retaliating women in both the trial and appeal (*Ellis* v. *R* 2003, 6). Crucially, however, 'normalisation' also involved the 'un-gendering' of domestic killing by comparing the murder of a female by her male partner, and even a man killing his ex-partner's lover, as if such killings are all the same (*Ellis* v. *R* 2003, 11). The unspoken implication is: there will always be a number of (ungendered) individuals who behave like that, this is unavoidable in intimate relationships, it is rare, but common enough to make it 'normal'. 'Normalisation of this kind . . . functions as a reassurance together with its counterpart . . . individualisation' (Mathiesen 2004, 26).

The third strategy is 'co-optation' – whatever aspect of the case raised concerns can be co-opted by emphasising it 'should be used as a point of departure for making further improvements of procedures which were all right earlier, but which may of course always be made better' (Mathiesen 2004, 27). This is exemplified in the new defence of 'diminished responsibility' introduced in 1957, frequently cited as being a direct consequence of the Ellis case (Goodman and Pringle 1974; Hancock 1989; Ballinger 1996), thus offering further reassurance to those who felt disturbed by her punishment.

Mathiesen's fourth strategy is 'superficial endorsement':

> 'Superficial endorsement' occurs when the criticism is too strong just to be punctured through individualisation, normalisation or co-optation. It is expressed through thoughtful and responsible – judiciously formulated – agreement that something particular is the matter and should be corrected.
>
> (2004, 27)

In the Ellis appeal the judges offered superficial endorsement to critics by noting that the law has *already* been corrected: 'If her crime were committed today, we think it likely that there would have been an issue of diminished responsibility for the jury to determine' (*Ellis* v. *R* 2003, 13).

Mathiesen's final strategy is that of 'displacement of responsibility' which 'implies that the responsibility in the area' will in future be placed on another agency and hence improve the system (2004, 28). It occurs when the implementation of the four previous strategies by themselves cannot reduce strong criticism and was exemplified in the Ellis case by the transference from judge to jury of the consideration of a diminished responsibility defence. Taken together, these five strategies prevent 'the public from being disturbed by thoughts of a somewhat more long-term character' (Mathiesen 2004, 29).

The Ellis case exemplifies the ebb and flow of hidden silencing, for while all five strategies were evident, they appeared to have limited success in silencing critics of the case, and arguably, at particular moments, carried the potential to generate a crisis of legitimacy. Ultimately, however, the Ellis appeal exemplifies the legal system's proficiency in bringing 'closure to controversial incidents' (Gilligan and Pratt 2004, 2), thus also demonstrating that the contest over knowledge between masculinist law and feminist epistemology is an unequal one. It also re-enforces Burton and Carlen's point discussed in relation to the Louie Calvert case, that the task of inquiries is to 're-establish the image of . . . legal coherence and rationality', thereby 'demonstrating the state's sovereign reason' as well as retaining confidence in key state apparatuses such as the legal system (1979, 48).

In short, 'the battle for truth' (Foucault 1980, 132) is not being fought between equals. Instead, as a result of its position at the top of the hierarchy of credibility legal discourse is able to construct 'an official, objective truth about crime, criminal justice and punishment' (Gilligan and Pratt 2004, 2), and it is this ability which closes the potential for the development of new subject positions. Within this context the Ellis appeal *strengthened* the case against her, and, in all likelihood, silently silenced her for the foreseeable future – paralysing our power of resistance in the process, and further ensuring that 'the prevailing [gender] order is maintained' (Mathiesen 2004, 19).

Conclusion

Following legal changes in Victoria, Australia in 2005 similar to those introduced in England and Wales in 2010 – the replacement of the provocation defence with 'loss of control' ('defensive homicide' in Victoria), Fitz-Gibbon and Pickering found that since its implementation, 'of the 15 convictions obtained for defensive homicide to date, only two have involved a female defendant', leading one judiciary member to comment: 'it is disturbing that defensive homicide has been resorted to by men in circumstances that the Law Reform Commission didn't really envisage.' Meanwhile, the Attorney-General observed that 'this law is not working as it's supposed to have worked and justice is not being served', while, anti-violence campaigners noted 'that the offence does not adequately address "the grim, gendered realities of family violence"' (Fitz-Gibbon and Pickering 2012, 166). Such testimonies led Fitz-Gibbon and Pickering to conclude that the new law of defensive homicide mirrors 'the problems previously associated with the defence of provocation' – thus, the legislation has changed but little 'has been achieved in practice' (2012, 167, 169).

Meanwhile in England and Wales, following the announcement by the Coroners and Justice Act in 2009 of the replacement of the provocation defence with 'loss of control' (effective from 4 October 2010), Edwards observes:

> Given that there is no change in the nomenclature, we can expect a mirror image of the behaviour and legal descriptors that passed for loss of self-control under the old law of provocation to be replicated.
>
> (2010, 224)

Moreover, the new law has returned the judge's 'power to remove cases from the jury's consideration' (Norrie in Edwards 2010, 240) – the very power which led to the collapse of Ruth's defence and subsequent omission of a closing speech.

Such developments confirm the validity of Smart's view that feminism should not become seduced by law – a new law will not make things better (1989, 160) – instead law itself should be de-centred in favour of a wider social context. This would allow a 'broader understanding of inequity, crime and responsibility and . . . would . . . review "the Law's" place at the top of the hierarchy in determining inequities and harms' (Morrissey 2003, 51). Without such a de-centring, law's superior position at the top of the hierarchy of truth production will be maintained and the continuity of 'hidden silencing' assured, as demonstrated by the outcome of the Ellis appeal.

6 A Victory for Injustice

Truth, Lies and Expert Knowledge – the Sally Clark Case

> [H]ow can verdicts be free from doubt when 'truths which yesterday have accomplished their deadly work upon an alleged criminal, may tomorrow be proclaimed as fallacies throughout the world of science'?
>
> (*Dublin University Magazine* (1856) in Ward 2004, 370)

Introduction

While the main focus in previous chapters has been law's ability to define the 'truth' through closing down new potential subject positions for generating alternative truths from experiential perspectives, the focus of this chapter is the symbiotic relationship between law and expert knowledge. Through the case-study of Sally Clark I shall demonstrate that when these two truth-producing bodies unite around the construction of official discourse, their combined force and power is of such magnitude that they also open up the danger and possibility, and in the Clark case, the reality, of generating a miscarriage of justice.

Having served more than three years of a life sentence for the murder of her two infant sons and gone through one failed appeal, Sally Clark was released from prison in January 2003, following a successful second appeal. Her case has subsequently been described as 'one of the greatest miscarriages of justices in recent times' (Osborne 2004, 1; Chapman and Broster 2003, 6), perhaps due to the fact that unlike many other notorious miscarriages of justice during recent decades, she had been found guilty of crimes which had never occurred – her children had died of natural causes. That these invented crimes – 'imaginary murders' – in the words of John Sweeney (in Batt 2004, 305) – could result in an innocent person receiving a life sentence and subsequently losing her appeal – was almost entirely a result of speculative, incompetent, misleading, and withholding of evidence by medical experts. Only after a thorough investigation by the Criminal Cases Review Commission (CCRC) was this gross miscarriage of justice finally recognised.

At a time of revolutionary developments within science and technology, where ground-breaking advances are taking place within forensic medicine, how could this have occurred? This chapter critically analyses this apparent contradiction by tracing the development of expert knowledge and its symbiotic – yet also potentially tempestuous – relationship with the legal system, and offers an in-depth feminist critique of both, the aim being to demonstrate that far from being based on scientific 'facts', expert knowledge – like other types of knowledge – is not only socially constructed, but also reinforces structures of patriarchal domination and subordination.

Furthermore, due to the relatively rare phenomenon of having gone through two appeals, the Sally Clark case offers an opportunity to expose the judiciary's ability to marshal the very same evidence to fit two outcomes in direct opposition to each other – in the first appeal to confirm her guilt – in the second, to indicate her innocence.

This chapter also continues to develop a key theme of the book – challenging a fundamental cornerstone of law – that its methods and tools have the ability to uncover an 'objective truth' which exists in isolation from human intervention or interference (Stanley and Wise 1993, 7). Instead, it argues that legal as well as medical arguments are socially constructed – built on shifting sands where the accused can easily find themselves in a situation of 'doomed if they do and doomed if they don't' (Raitt and Zeedyk 2004, 270) – that is to say – available evidence can be made to fit whichever scenario is being proposed. It is therefore not surprising that the courts' pursuit of mothers who have lost children due to Sudden Infant Death Syndrome (SIDS) or other unascertained causes, has repeatedly been described as a witch-hunt – reminiscent of medieval reasoning where 'one is guilty until one can prove that one is not guilty, and one has no way in which to prove that one is not guilty' (Mar in Raitt and Zeedyk 2004, 270).

Finally, the chapter emphasises the gendered aspect of this contemporary witch-hunt that has resulted in accusations of 'imaginary murder', for, as noted in the previous chapter, in an era where women have been largely successful in establishing *legal* equality with men, it is nevertheless the case that particular discourses of femininity continue to make their impact felt in such trials – albeit in a far more oblique manner than in previous eras – a characteristic which serves to increase their insidiousness. As observed by Raitt and Zeedyk in relation to the cases of Sally Clark and Angela Cannings,[1] these discourses 'operated subtly, and thus all the more influentially' (2004, 267).

The Case

At 11 weeks old, Christopher Clark, the first-born son of Sally and Stephen Clark, died suddenly during the evening of 13 December 1996. A *post mortem* was carried out by Home Office pathologist Dr Alan Williams, who considered the cause of death to be a 'lower respiratory tract infection'; the death was subsequently

1 Angela Cannings was convicted of smothering two of her children in 2002. Export knowledge in the form of Professor Meadow's testimony had formed an important part of the prosecution's case. Cannings was released in 2003 after her appeal was upheld (Campbell and Walker undated, 19–20).

'treated as a case of SIDS' (*R* v. *Clark* 2000, para2). While Dr Williams also found bruises on the body and a small split in the frenulum, 'he considered that these findings were consistent with *minor* harm caused during the resuscitation attempts' (*R* v. *Clark* 2003, para8, emphasis added).

When the Clark's second son, Harry, was born in November 1997, the couple enrolled into the Care of Next Infant programme (CONI), which resulted in him being closely monitored, especially during the night, when he was attached to an apnoea alarm. He died unexpectedly in January 1998, at eight weeks old. Dr Williams also performed Harry's *post mortem* examination and concluded that 'shaking was the likely cause of death' because he had 'found injuries which he considered to be indicative of non-accidental injury, consistent with episodes of shaking on several occasions over several days' (*R* v. *Clark* 2003, para10).

As a direct consequence of his conclusion, Williams re-visited his own findings in relation to Christopher's death and subsequently considered them to be inaccurate. He now maintained that 'the injury to the frenulum could be *interpreted* as the mouth having been obstructed or smothered' (*R* v. *Clark* 2000, para28, emphasis added). Moreover, although neither ambulance nor hospital staff had noticed *any* bruises on Christopher's body, 'he was in no doubt they were bruises', and contrary to his original findings, 'he was satisfied they had been caused before death' (*R* v. *Clark* 2000, para30). Thus, after consulting with an eye specialist, Professor Green, who claimed he had found evidence which made trauma 'a serious possibility' and 'a very strong probability' (*R* v. *Clark* 2000, para58), Williams now concluded that Christopher had been smothered. This led to the arrest in February 1998 of Sally and Stephen Clark on suspicion of Harry's murder. By April, charges against Stephen were dropped. However, Sally was now also suspected of having murdered Christopher (*R* v. *Clark* 2003, paras10–13).

The Trial

> It cannot be said too often that an English criminal trial is not a search for objective truth. It is a game in which the player with the strongest hand will probably win. Is 1: 73 million a trump card?
>
> (Batt 2004, 146)

> My honest, law-abiding family has just been crushed by the machinery of the State.
>
> (Stephen Clark in Batt 2004, 207)

A key argument presented by the prosecution was that the two deaths shared factors which 'went far beyond coincidence':

i Christopher and Harry were about the same age at death namely 11 and 8 weeks.
ii They were both discovered unconscious by Mrs Clark in the bedroom, allegedly both in a bouncy chair.

iii Both were found at about 9.30 in the evening, shortly after having taken a successful feed.
iv Mrs Clark had been alone with each child when he was discovered lifeless.
v In each case Mr Clark was either away or about to go away from home in connection with his work.
vi In each case there was evidence consistent with previous abuse.
vii In each case there was evidence consistent with recently inflicted deliberate injury.

(*R* v. *Clark* 2003, para14)

The medical evidence relied upon by the prosecution was complex, yet vague and contradictory, with experts called to support Dr Williams's claim that Harry had been shaken, but offering little or no evidence of this theory. For example, Professor Green, the eye specialist whose evidence had played a pivotal role in Dr Williams changing his mind as to the cause of death of Christopher prior to the trial, now 'accepted [with respect to Harry] that what he initially thought was intra-retinal haemorrhaging, was due to an error in the slide preparation and he was now satisfied the bleeding had occurred post mortem' (*R* v. *Clark* 2000, para54). Indeed, 'features commonly associated with shaking, such as contusional tears, damage to the cervical cord and subdural haemorrhage, were not present here' (*R* v. *Clark* 2000, para58). Thus, despite being a prosecution witness, he gave the cause of death as 'unascertained'[2] (*R* v. *Clark* 2000, para33).

Another expert, Dr Smith, stated there was no 'swelling in the brain, nor did she see any tears of the brain unequivocally caused before death':

> There was *no indisputable evidence of traumatic injury*, but . . . small haemorrhages on the surface of the brain . . . which *could* have been caused by direct injury or stoppage of oxygen. She also found signs of hypoxic damage to nerve cells due to lack of oxygen before death. Such damage *could* be caused *if* the airways were obstructed . . . Although the beta APP staining process had revealed *no recent damage* where trauma might have been expected . . . she concluded that *some* hours before Harry's death *something* had happened, which caused damage to the nerve cells in the brain.
>
> (*R* v. *Clark* 2000, para54, emphasis added)

Moreover, while she had found evidence of bleeding in the epidural space, she also agreed

> this was not one of the usual findings in a shaken baby and was unable to say what mechanism had caused it. She had never regarded this case as a classic

2 The standard term employed by the medical profession when a cause of death cannot be established.

> shaking case and she did not think it was a case where there had been a direct thump to the child.
>
> (*R* v. *Clark* 2000, para57)

A third expert, Dr Keeling, testified that:

> the damage did not give *any indication of causality, but one possible cause was trauma* . . . *If* something else had occurred, it was another insult very close to death, which *probably* would not have been seen on the beta protein staining process.
>
> (*R* v. *Clark* 2000, para55, emphasis added)

Yet, she also testified that 'there was no damage to the cervical part of the spine, and no evidence of traumatic damage to the brain. She could not say what had triggered the bleeding in the epidural space' (*R* v. *Clark* 2000, para60). Like Professor Green, Dr Keeling, also a prosecution witness, gave the cause of death as 'unascertained' (*R* v. *Clark* 2000, para33). Conversely, Dr Berry 'thought the timing of the deaths was unusual but not very unusual for a SIDS death' (*R* v. *Clark* 2000, para145).

As each and every expert called failed to find evidence to support Williams's claim that Harry had been shaken, the prosecution's case 'shifted away from shaking towards smothering' (*R* v. *Clark* 2000, para88). Dr Williams, however, attempting to sustain his diagnosis of shaken-baby-syndrome, also claimed to have discovered a fractured rib:

> In his statement, he had referred to it as a 'possible' old fracture, but in evidence he was adamant that there was no other explanation [for his finding]. He had told DI Gardner that it could have been a birth injury, but that was only so that he could investigate other possibilities . . . He had not included it in his post mortem findings because it was of unknown significance.
>
> (*R* v. *Clark* 2000, para61)

During cross-examination Williams conceded that

> the fracture did not show up on X-ray . . . [that] he never saw the fractured rib, only felt it. Nobody saw it. The fracture was nearly healed . . . Although it is his normal practice, he cannot remember if he photographed it. He has not seen such a photo.
>
> (Batt 2004, 116–17)

He further conceded that 'this child does not show the features one expects to see in the head of a shaken baby' (Batt 2004, 115).

It was acknowledged that a fractured rib would have been extremely painful for a baby to endure, yet Harry was regularly seen by health visitors and had been to the baby clinic the very day of his death, as well as having accompanied his mother to her GP, yet, no medical staff had at any time noticed Harry being in discomfort. On the contrary, they described him as being well cared for. The Clarks' nanny had also failed to notice either bruises or any form of discomfort when handling Harry and considered Sally 'to be a loving, caring mother' (*R* v. *Clark* 2000, para43).

With respect to Christopher's death, Dr Williams initially noted in his post-mortem report: 'Lung – acute inflammation; spleen – focal haemorrhages and inflammation; tonsils/pharaynxes – minor inflammation' and thus concluded 'the cause of death was . . . lower respiratory tract infection'. However, by the time of the trial, Dr Williams had dismissed infection as the cause of death, and instead explained that 'there was a "possibility that the child was smothered . . . a possibility in a broad range"' (cited in *R* v. *Clark* 2003, para57). To further support this 'possibility', he claimed to have found 'bleeding in the lungs', but 'he had made no reference to this finding because he considered it was "part of the dying process" and "a non specific finding"' (cited in *R* v. *Clark* 2003, para42).

As had been the case with respect to Williams' findings concerning the cause of Harry's death, other experts were not prepared to unequivocally support this new cause of death with respect to Christopher. Thus, when the trial concluded, only one other expert supported Dr Williams in his claim that these deaths were unnatural, *all* other defence *and* prosecution expert witnesses agreed that the causes of death were unascertained.

This other expert was Professor Sir Roy Meadow, who gained notoriety with his claim that in a family like the Clarks',[3] there was a 1 in 8,543 risk of one SIDS. Therefore, in order to calculate what the chances are of two SIDS occurring in one such family 'you have to multiply 1 in 8,543 times 1 in 8,543 . . . it's approximately a chance of 1 in 73 million':

> in England, Wales and Scotland there are about say 700,000 live births a year, so it is saying by chance that happening will occur once every hundred years.
> (Meadow cited in *R* v. *Clark* 2003, para96)

These statistics were not only utterly inaccurate (see below) but also entirely irrelevant since neither Sally nor her defence claimed the babies had died of SIDS. Meadow's evidence could thus be considered prejudicial and should, arguably, have been inadmissible (Batt 2004, 151–2).[4] Instead, Meadow added:

> it's the chance of backing that long odds outsider at the Grand National, you know; let's say it's a 80 to 1 chance, you back the winner last year, then the next year there's another horse at 80 to 1 and it is still 80 to 1 and you back it again, and it wins. Now here we're in a situation that, you know, to get to

3 The Clark family were in a low risk category due to the fact they were non-smokers; there was a wage-earner in the family and the mother was over 26 years old (*R* v. *Clark* 2003 para96).

4 In fact, this statistic was eventually considered inadmissible by the time of the second appeal (Skeleton Argument, 16).

> these odds of 73 million you've got to back that 1 in 80 chance four years running, so yes, you might be very, very lucky because each time it's just been a 1 in 80 chance and you know, you've happened to have won it, but the chance of it happening four years running we all know is extraordinarily unlikely. So it's the same with these deaths. You have to say two unlikely events have happened and together it's very, very, very unlikely.
>
> (Meadow cited in *R* v. *Clark* 2003, para99)

Conversely, it was never suggested by either the prosecution or defence that this might be a case of Munchausen's Syndrome by Proxy (MSbP), a condition discovered by Professor Meadow, yet he was allowed to provide elaborate details about his research on this subject – the emphasis being on mothers who harm their children. As observed by Batt, a consultant to Sally's defence team, 'it has no relevance, it is inadmissible' (2004, 127); it was nonetheless presented to the jury.

When invited to provide further scientific support to indicate the Clark babies had been killed rather than died naturally, Meadow offered these insights:

> The peak period . . . is between midnight and 11a.m. The baby is put to sleep. The parents get up, often rather latish and to their tremendous sadness they find the baby dead at nine, ten in the morning . . . that's the normal circumstance of natural sudden death . . . For . . . unnatural deaths, the commonest time for them to die was in the late afternoon/evening. Parents, when asleep, don't kill their children so it would have been surprising if the findings were otherwise. Child abuse is commonest at that time, they're often at their most annoying.
>
> (cited in Batt 2004, 128–9; *R* v. *Clark* 2000, para32)

Yet, even Professor Meadow, whose statistical evidence arguably was to prove decisive in the jury's return of a guilty verdict, conceded 'there was a lack of research on shaking of babies and it was *no more than guess work*' (*R* v. *Clark* 2000, para59, emphasis added).

The only trial witness not hired by either prosecution or defence was Dr David, appointed by the Family Division Court as an independent expert. He considered that death may have been caused by haemosiderosis, a suggestion dismissed by Professor Meadow (*R* v. *Clark* 2000, para27). Dr David further found 'there was no evidence that the haemorrhages were due to abuse' and that 'there was insufficient data to know why Harry died' (*R* v. *Clark* 2000, paras75; 77).

The First Appeal

> where judicial institutions and medical knowledge, or scientific knowledge in general, intersect, statements are formulated having the status of true discourses with considerable judicial effects. However, these statements also have the curious property . . . of being, in the strict sense, grotesque.
>
> (Foucault 2003, 11)

> It is the most intellectually dishonest appeal judgement I have ever read.
>
> (Bevan in Batt 2004, 236)

The first ground for the appeal argued that the trial judge had been wrong to deny Sally separate trials for the two counts of murder. The appeal judges dismissed this ground by reiterating the seven similarities outlined above, which indicated that an 'explanation based on coincidence offends common sense' (*R* v. *Clark* 2000, para81).

A second ground was the misuse of statistics by Meadow which had resulted in the prosecution inviting

> the jury to adopt the figure of 73 million as having a significance in itself . . . Consequently, the jury were led to believe that this evidence demonstrated that the chances of the appellant being innocent was a least 73 million to 1 against.
>
> (*R* v. *Clark* 2000, para168)

The appeal judges did not accept Meadow had misused statistics, however, they conceded that 'he did not help to explain their limited significance' and that the figure of 1:73 million was 'merely a distraction' (*R* v. *Clark* 2000, paras178, 179). Nonetheless, while there was 'some substance' to this ground, the use of statistics 'was very much a side-show at trial' and as such, did not render the conviction unsafe (*R* v. *Clark* 2000, paras184, 142).

A third ground for the appeal centred on the credibility of Dr Williams' evidence. As noted, above, none of the experts unequivocally supported his claim that the haemorrhages in Harry's eyes indicated smothering. Instead, they were thought to have occurred *post mortem*. When the defence finally succeeded in obtaining the notes for the cases on which Dr Williams had based his findings, they consisted of three cases which he had examined *after* Sally's trial. The defence argued they 'were not comparable' with Harry's case (*R* v. *Clark* 2000, para78d). Yet, they 'had a serious impact upon one aspect of Dr Williams' evidence and moreover [would] inevitably have affected the jury's assessment of Dr Williams' reliability' (*R* v. *Clark* 2000, para212). The appeal judges disagreed, stating that 'references to the haemorrhages . . . played a minor role' in the summing up (*R* v. *Clark* 2000, para208). If anything, '*the fresh evidence is capable of affirming rather than undermining the credibility of Dr Williams*' (*R* v. *Clark* 2000, para239, emphasis added). To support this claim, the judges quoted three expert witnesses who 'all agreed that, although they had *never seen* such haemorrhages, *nor read about them*, and therefore Harry was unique, nevertheless the haemorrhages, *if real*, were in conjunction with the other haemorrhages consistent with smothering' (*R* v. *Clark* 2000, para223, emphasis added).

Thus, having concluded that 'there is substance in only one of the grounds of appeal, namely that relating to the statistical evidence', the appeal judges stated that 'the recurrent features of infant killing . . . identified by Professor Meadow, were present' (*R* v. *Clark* 2000, para257), and 'provided the jury accepted

Dr Williams's evidence' with respect to Christopher's death (*R* v. *Clark* 2000, para256), these features formed part of the 'overwhelming evidence of the guilt of the appellant on each count' (*R* v. *Clark* 2000, para254). The appeal was therefore dismissed.

The Second Appeal

> Throughout my review, I was horrified by the shoddy fashion in which these cases were evaluated. It was clear that sound medical principles were abandoned in favour of oversimplifications, over-interpretations, exclusion of relevant data and, in several instances, the imagining of non-existent findings.
>
> (Dr Gullino cited in Batt 2004, 109; Report on Second Appeal)

Sally's family never accepted her guilt, and following the dismissal of her appeal, Stephen Clark succeeded in retrieving test results of Harry's blood which had not been disclosed at either the trial or the first appeal. The report indicated Harry had suffered from an infection

> that had spread as far as [his] cerebral spinal fluid (CSF). This led to an investigation by the CCRC who referred the case back to the Court of Appeal. The non disclosure of the report became the first ground of the Appeal. The tests had been ordered by Dr Williams who had known the results 'since February 1998. He had kept the results secret . . . '.
>
> (Skeleton Argument [henceforth SA] 2003, 1)

After disclosure of these results, experts who had given evidence during the trial now confirmed the crucial impact this infection would have had on the cause of death. Professor Berry stated it 'would have had a significant impact on his opinion as to the cause of Harry's death' (SA 2003, 3). Dr Rushton 'concluded on the basis of the reports now available . . . that the death of Harry was due to staphylococcal infection' (SA 2003, 4). Professor Luthert – one of the experts the appeal judges had referred to as having provided 'overwhelming evidence' of Sally's guilt (*R* v. *Clark* 2000, para223) – 'described the situation on non disclosure as "blood chilling"' (SA 2003, 4). He was one of several experts to confirm that in the light of the new disclosure, evidence which had previously been presented to indicate Sally had harmed Harry – for example haemorrhages in the eyes and swollen cord/bleeding in the cervical space – were likely to have arisen in connection with this infection (SA 2003, 4). Professor David, the court appointed expert whose conclusion that Harry had died of natural causes had been dismissed by Professor Meadow, voiced his disbelief at the non-disclosure:

> What is so extraordinary is that these results were obviously of special interest to the pathology department . . . and yet . . . none of the results were disclosed . . . I am at a loss to understand how all these results . . . did not come to be passed into the care proceedings papers . . . had these results been

> available, I would have . . . investigated their possible significance further not only in relation to the death of Harry but also the death of Christopher.
>
> (SA 2003, 4)

In short, the newly disclosed report had a grave impact upon the interpretations and *mis*interpretations of evidence presented at the trial, much of which could now be traced to natural causes with regard to Harry and which *had initially* been traced to natural causes with respect to Christopher. Thus, questions were now asked as to the credibility of Dr Williams in view of his failure to disclose such important evidence. His competence and impartiality was of outmost importance since 'the majority of the critical points in the prosecution case depend upon disputed and inadequately documented "findings" by Dr Williams' (SA 2003, 6). Thus, factors vi) and vii) amongst the list of factors which the first appeal judges referred to as being 'far beyond coincidence' (see above), were by far the most serious, because they claimed evidence of 'previous abuse' and 'deliberate injury' – yet they also relied entirely on Williams' findings which the second appeal judges found unconvincing. For example, they noted that his claim to have seen bruises on Christopher's body 'was purely from his observations and had not been confirmed by incision' or indeed by any other witness or medical staff (*R* v. *Clark* 2003, paras32–33). With respect to the small split into the frenulum:

> the existence of such an injury should have been put beyond question by photographs, but . . . the photographs that were taken were . . . of very poor quality and offered no opportunity for others to assess the finding Dr Williams claimed to have made.
>
> (*R* v. *Clark* 2003, para35)

Moreover, with regard to his change of diagnosis as to the cause of Christopher's death, Dr Williams had shown a lack of awareness of 'possible diagnostic relevance[s], it suggests that Dr Williams was being selective as to his recording of his findings only recording those facts that seemed to him to be supportive of his conclusion' (*R* v. *Clark* 2003, para42).

> As already made clear Dr Williams immediately after Christopher's death considered that he had died from a lower respiratory tract infection. By the date of trial not only had Dr Williams changed his diagnosis as to the likely cause of death but somewhat more surprisingly he went so far as to rule out such an infection as a possible cause of death.
>
> (*R* v. *Clark* 2003, para52)

The judges concluded 'that he advanced no convincing explanation for the alteration of his position . . . Put at its very lowest, this aspect of the matter called into question the competence of Dr Williams' (*R* v. *Clark* 2003, para55). This conclusion was reinforced by the fact that any evidence Harry had died naturally carried special significance because:

> The evidence in respect of Christopher's death, if it stood in isolation would not have justified a finding of murder and if, therefore there had been evidence that suggested that Harry died from natural causes . . . it seems inevitably to follow that [the jury] could not have been sure that Christopher was murdered.
>
> (*R* v. *Clark* 2003, para93)

With these grave consequences in mind, the second appeal judges reflected on Williams' behaviour:

> It is clear that Dr Williams appreciated that this was information that needed to be considered before a final conclusion was reached on the cause of Harry's death . . . However, [he] made no reference to these results, not even to having submitted these samples for examination.
>
> (*R* v. *Clark* 2003, paras140, 142)

Instead, Williams had categorically stated that 'there is no evidence of acute infection . . . There is no evidence that this child died as a result of natural disease' (*R* v. *Clark* 2003, para146). The failure to refer to these results was variously described as 'astonishing', 'an "error of judgement"' and 'substandard practice' by other experts (*R* v. *Clark* 2003, paras151; 152). Moreover, having heard evidence that tests had been carried out on Christopher which led to Williams's original conclusion that he had died of respiratory infection, the jury had specifically asked: 'Are there blood tests for Harry?' (*R* v. *Clark* 2003, para156). The prosecutor at the trial – not being aware of the tests either – had replied: 'As I understand it, the answer is that there was no blood sample taken for chemical analysis . . . in the case of Harry as there was for Christopher' (*R* v. *Clark* 2003, para157). Still not satisfied, the jury asked why there was no analysis of Harry's blood 'for comparison' and was again told 'that a sample was not collected from Harry to measure the chemical in his blood' (*R* v. *Clark* 2003, paras158, 159).

Thus, there had been specific opportunities for Dr Williams to correct this misinformation during the trial. His failure to do so led the appeal judges to conclude that 'he had fallen a very long way short of standards to be expected of someone in his position upon whose evidence the court was inevitably going to be so dependent' (*R* v. *Clark* 2003, para164). Given the severity of their criticism they offered 'him the opportunity . . . to explain his apparent shortcomings' – he declined do so (*R* v. *Clark* 2003, para165; Nobles and Schiff 2004, 239). Hence, only his written statement, in which he outlined his normal practice, was available to the judges who responded:

> We find that explanation wholly unacceptable . . . on the evidence available to us his practice is completely out of line with the practice accepted by other pathologists to be the standard. It is likely to mislead others . . . who will be denied the opportunity of considering the material in the way that Dr Williams explained that he found necessary, in reaching their own properly

> informed conclusion. 'If I can discount it, nobody else need consider it.' As an approach it only has to be voiced for the inherent danger to be obvious.
>
> (*R* v. *Clark* 2003, para167)

The lack of professionalism which played a large role in causing this miscarriage of justice was eloquently summed up by Professor Byard:

> Standard protocols were not followed and essential steps such as routine dissection and histology were omitted which prevented verification of alleged autopsy findings. . . . A number of potentially important diagnoses and conclusions were altered over time. For example, Christopher's initial cause of death of lower respiratory tract infection was withdrawn, observations of no significant haemorrhage within his lungs were changed to marked haemorrhage . . . The finding of retinal haemorrhages in Harry which was vital to sustain the diagnosis of shaken-impact syndrome was altered to no haemorrhage, brain lacerations were found to represent post-mortem artefact, swelling of the spinal cord was not present and bruising of paraspinal tissues was also not able to be substantiated.
>
> (*R* v. *Clark* 2003, para169)

The judges upheld the appeal on the non-disclosure of evidence alone, but chose to respond to what would have been a second ground – had it been necessary – Professor Meadow's statistical evidence. They agreed with the first appeal judges that he had failed to qualify his statistics which themselves represented an 'illegitimate over-simplification' of the chances of two SIDS deaths occurring in one family (*R* v. *Clark* 2003, para102). However, they went further than the first appeal judges, noting: 'The jury were required to return separate verdicts on the two counts but the 1 in 73 million figure encouraged consideration of the two counts together as a package' (*R* v. *Clark* 2003, para173). Moreover, if this figure had been a accurate reflection of 'the chance of two cot deaths in the same family, then the whole of the CONI scheme was effectively wasted effort', since the entire point of its existence was to advise already bereaved parents how to avoid a second death (*R* v. *Clark* 2003, para176).

Furthermore, the judges took a more critical view of the factors of 'similarity' which went 'far beyond coincidence' according to the first appeal judges. It will be recalled that apart from the final two factors already discussed above which depended on Dr Williams's evidence, the remaining five were all factors devised by Professor Meadow to support his claim of child abuse and murder. The judges found these 'similarities' unacceptable: 'We fail to see how realistically on the facts of this case they can be thought to be any significant indication of murder' (*R* v. *Clark* 2000, para15). Thus, it was hardly surprising the children had died while in their mother's sole care, knowing that it is overwhelmingly mothers who take the main responsibility for childcare. Furthermore, 'it is difficult to see how any sort of adverse conclusion could properly be drawn simply from the fact that one died at 8 weeks old and the other at 11 weeks old', or the fact that Stephen had been out the night Christopher died, and was going away the day after Harry's death. 'We cannot accept [this indicated more than] ordinary incidence of family life' (*R* v. *Clark* 2003, para15). As to the 'similarity' that both children had taken a 'successful feed' shortly before death – this was inaccurate. Dr Williams' own report stated there was 'no evidence of a recent meal' in Harry's stomach, unsurprisingly so, since there *was* evidence he had vomited before death, a 'potentially important finding . . . [which] appears not to have been put before the jury' (*R* v. *Clark* 2003, para16).

Finally, 'there was no evidence that anyone had noticed any injury to either child during their lives . . . Such evidence as there was suggested they were babies who were well cared for, loved by their parents and happy and content'. Within this context, the accuracies of expert testimonies were crucial, since the case rested solely on 'medical evidence . . . and particularly upon the evidence of the pathologists' (*R* v. *Clark* 2003, para17). Consequently, the second appeal was upheld.

The blatant professional misconduct of key expert witnesses in the Sally Clark case arguably offered the opportunity to individualise the 'cause' of this miscarriage of justice. That is, identifying rogue individuals as being the sole culprits allows the wider legal structures within which experts like Williams and Meadow operated to remain unexplored. In turn, this can be understood as contributing towards the stability of the legal process at a time when it potentially faced a crisis of legitimacy. After briefly re-visiting feminist critiques of expert knowledge, the remainder of this chapter challenges this individualisation by considering the wider structural and theoretical issues arising from this miscarriage of justice.

The Feminist Challenge to Expert Knowledge Revisited

> It is true that expert . . . opinion contributes nothing to knowledge, but this is not what matters. Its essential role is to legitimize, in the form of scientific knowledge, the extension of punitive power to something that is not a breach of the law.
>
> (Foucault 2003, 18)

The roots of expert knowledge were traced in Chapter 2 to the founding principles of the Enlightenment – those of science, rationality, reason and objectivity. Enlightenment philosophy advocated that these principles are the correct tools for determining the accuracy of knowledge and uncover 'the truth', a philosophy which allows scientific knowledge to be positioned at the apex of the hierarchy of credibility.

It was further argued in Chapter 2, that while law is not a science, it is nonetheless able to construct itself as if it is, setting 'itself apart from and above other discourses in the same way that science does', by also claiming to be based in rationality and objectivity which ensures its ability to arrive at the 'true' interpretation of events, to the point where it claims to have 'direct access to the truth which avoids the problem of human interpretation' (Smart 1995, 73, 74).

This claim allows scientific experts to construct themselves as standing outside the social order as a result of an apparent rigorous implementation of these 'objective' and 'value-free' scientific methods and procedures. As explained in Chapter 2, they are constructed as appropriate judges to assess, diagnose and recognise 'the normal and abnormal', they are 'the judges of normality' (Foucault 1977, 304). Moreover, Foucault's observation that judges possess an 'immense "appetite for medicine" . . . constantly manifested from their appeal to psychiatric experts' (1977, 304), is particularly relevant to the Sally Clark case, because it identifies the symbiotic relationship between law and medico-scientific experts whose absence in the courtroom during murder trials have become virtually unthinkable – such is the key role they play in court cases involving serious crime.

As noted above, the feminist challenge to such claims of 'scientificity', objectivity and value-neutrality has taken the form of exposing them as self-serving social constructions, because a claim to truth is in fact 'a claim to deploy power' (Smart 1995, 72). That is to say, 'the authority to identify "empirical truths" and to interpret observable, testable "facts" is dependent on existing power relations within given social contexts' (Faith in Ballinger 2003, 219). In this way feminist critiques revealed that knowledge which had hitherto been accepted as 'scientific' and 'objective' was 'intimately tied to relations of dominance and exclusion' (Letherby 2003, 59), and as such, inherently masculinist and heteropatriarchal in nature. The social construction of expert knowledge had thus become exposed, allowing further critiques to be developed in relation to 'traditional, biologically determined, "scientific" explanations of female behaviour in general, and their criminality in particular' (Ballinger 2011, 109).

Moreover, in a culture that values scientific knowledge above other forms of knowledge, defining a field as 'science' carries the potential to accrue substantial power through disqualifying already subjugated knowledge such as lived experience, beliefs and opinions generated outside scientific discourses (Smart 1995, 73). Additionally, when operating within the legal system, these claims to 'scientificity' and 'truth' disguise and mystify the subjugation and transformation of the defendant's own account.

The feminist challenge to legal theory and practice, together with critiques of the symbiotic relationship between law and expert knowledge (Smart 1989; Heidensohn 1986; Allen 1987b; Ballinger 2005), has demonstrated how traditional phallocentric knowledge about women can have specific and immensely detrimental consequences for female defendants, because they are judged, not only according to their crimes, but also according to standards of femininity. Within this context feminists have identified those women who fail to fulfil gender role expectations and who also break the law as 'doubly deviant,' as demonstrated in the Louie Calvert case above (Smart and Smart 1978, 3; Morris 1987; Naffine 1990; Kennedy 1993; Ballinger 2000). In short, second-wave feminism posed challenges to the nature of knowledge production itself, which underpins the very foundations on which 'truth' is established within the courtroom, and which therefore can have far-reaching consequences for the defendant. The following sections highlight how those specific aspects of feminist analysis are relevant to the Sally Clark case.

Reinforcing Guilt: The Role of Expert Knowledge

> Meadow's Law, in the ascendant for far too long, is at last exposed for what it is – a nasty little slogan coined in bad faith, bad taste, bad law and bad science.
>
> (Orr 2003, 21)

The first issue to be explored is the role of the symbiotic relationship between law and expert knowledge in the violation of the fundamental legal principle 'presumption of innocence until proven guilty'. The very foundation upon which the prosecution based its case stood in direct conflict with this principle, because it consisted of little more than Meadow's alleged 'similarities' outlined above, which were claimed to go 'far beyond coincidence'. Based on that claim:

> They submitted that in such circumstances where there was no evidence in each case to suggest that the child had died from natural causes, the inference could safely be drawn that the death resulted from the act of the person in whose care the child was when he suddenly became unwell.
>
> (*R* v. *Clark* 2003, para14)

Combined with 'Meadow's Law' that 'unless proven otherwise, one cot death is a tragedy and two is suspicious and three is murder' – 'his theory reverses the simple test of justice – that someone is innocent until proven guilty' (Sweeney 2003, 27). Given his role as key expert for the prosecution, it is perhaps no coincidence that extensive discussion of MSbP was heard by the jury, for he was the inventor of this condition in the 1970s and the Royal College of Paediatrics and Child Health for which he was president noted in its guidelines on MSbP that 'some forensic pathologists advise that one should begin with the assumption that every unexpected infant death is due to homicide' (cited in Raitt and Zeedyk 2004, 271). Thus, although MSbP was irrelevant to the case, constructing an association with it can be understood as an example of Foucault's 'extenuating circumstances'[5] – how details not relevant to the case are revealed during 'the production of judicial truth', for the purposes of proving a person's guilt (Foucault 2003, 11). Indeed, Meadow's five points of similarities utilised 'as evidence of similar fact' – and dismissed as irrelevant during the second appeal – also fit into the category of 'extenuating circumstances', because they exemplify the way in which expert opinion

> allows the offence . . . to be doubled with a whole series of other things that are not the offence itself but a series of forms of conduct, of ways of being

5 Foucault explains that the purpose of 'extenuating circumstances' is 'not to allow a softening of the penalty'; rather its objective is to prevent juries from *not* convicting in cases where there is evidence but no certainty. Although he identifies its frequent use within the legal system, he also states it is an illegal concept since if there is no certainty the jury must find the defendant innocent (2003, 9).

> that are . . . presented in the discourse of the . . . expert as the cause, origin, motivation and starting point of the offence.
>
> (Foucault 2003, 15)

Expert opinion can thus recount a series of events which do not break the law – babies dying at a similar age; being alone with their mother when they died; having been fed prior to their death; husband away or about to go away – the aim being 'to show how the individual already resembles his crime before he has committed it' (Foucault 2003, 19; Downing 2013, 8).

The first appeal judges interacted with medical experts in a further example of Foucault's 'doubling' of the offence when they drew attention to Sally's reaction to her baby's death:

> The behaviour of the appellant at hospital when told her baby was dead impressed Dr Douglas as ' . . . very dramatic and almost hysterical . . . ' and was described by her as ' . . . such an over-reaction'.
>
> (*R* v. *Clark* 2000, para258)

Notwithstanding the problematic nature of defining what constitutes a mother's 'over-reaction' to her baby's sudden death, presumably, if Sally had *failed* to show a reaction to the death of her baby, that too would have been interpreted as problematic behaviour. However, neither over- nor under-reaction is legitimate *evidence of guilt*. As observed by Raitt and Zeedyk, 'any behaviour can be twisted so that it appears to have an alternative meaning', yet Dr Douglas's 'assessment was considered a key piece of evidence in Clark's original conviction and . . . first appeal' (2004, 270, 272). Similar importance was attributed to a remark by Sally to the coroner that she and Stephen hoped to become parents again in the future. The coroner 'felt that it was unusual to express a wish for another child' so soon after losing a baby (cited in Raitt and Zeedyk 2004, 272). Again Foucault reminds us that such behaviour is not illegal. However:

> expert opinion allows one to pass from action to conduct, from an offence to a way of being and to make this way of being appear as nothing other than the offence itself . . . [it] is a kind of reconstruction of the crime itself, in a scaled down version, before it has been committed. In short, the function of expert opinion is to double the author of the crime, whether responsible or not, with a delinquent who is the object of a specific technology.
>
> (2003, 16, 19, 20, 21)

Finally, the first appeal judges noted that 'she had no credible account in respect of the previous injuries sustained by each baby' (*R* v. *Clark* 2000, para255). Notwithstanding that the second appeal revealed these 'injuries' had been manufactured by Williams, hence, it was unsurprising that Sally was unable to explain their origin, it served as yet another example of the violation of the concept of 'presumed innocent', since it is not a requirement of defendants to prove their innocence; rather, it is for the prosecution to prove their guilt.

The pursuit of Sally and other bereaved mothers through the courts based on such violation of a cornerstone of law – presumption of innocence – explains why such trials have been termed witch-hunts. It also goes to the heart of the feminist critique of expert knowledge, for far from being objective, neutral or value-free, Meadow exemplifies a category of experts known as the 'think dirty brigade' (Vasager and Allison 2003, 3), a term which reflects their predisposal to formulate highly subjective, guilt-presumptive opinions and judgements about bereaved mothers:

> he comes to any case with the prior belief, if you believe somebody has murdered a baby there is no way in which you can prove she hasn't. If she is alone in the house with a baby and the baby has died, there's no evidence that the pathologist can give, there's no evidence she can produce that proves that she hasn't done it and therefore it's very easy to throw that suspicion.
>
> (Golding cited in *File on Four* 2002, 4)

Even *after* the conviction was secured, Foucault's 'doubling' of the crime continued – this time by the prosecutor who, having been under a court order not to mention Sally's history with alcohol during the trial, now stated:

> I think it right that the full facts of the case be made known now and I take this opportunity to make clear that it would have formed part of the prosecution's case that alcohol played a part in that it was so serious that Mrs Clark was treated for it at the Priory.
>
> (cited in Batt 2004, 208)

Notwithstanding the fact that *no* alcohol was involved at the time of the babies' deaths – hence, the prosecutor's statement was inaccurate – arguably, raising this issue served to reinforce perceived weaknesses in Sally's character, in order to emphasise the likelihood of her guilt, thus adding legitimacy to the majority verdict. Deliberately drawing attention to Sally's history with alcohol has particular gendered significance, for while excessive drinking by male defendants may be utilised as a *mitigating* circumstance, the situation is reversed in cases of female defendants (Finch and Munro 2007, 593). Thus, as a result of this pointless revelation by the prosecutor since a guilty verdict had already been returned, Sally had to endure the added informal punishment of personal details being revealed in newspapers like the *Daily Mail*, despite the fact they were already in the past at the time of the children's birth: 'it can be revealed that Clark suffered severe problems with alcoholism and depression, which left her career in tatters' (cited in Nobles and Schiff 2004, 231).

Unscientific Science

> Some evidence has in itself an effect of power, a demonstrative value, greater than other evidence and independently of its own rational structure. To what is this effect due if it is not the rational structure of the evidence? Well, it is due to the status of the subject who presents the evidence.
>
> (Foucault 2003, 10)

> Meadow's Law is 'scientifically illiterate'.
>
> (Drucker in Sweeney and Law 2003, 8)

The second issue to be explored is the myth of science. The gap between myth and reality in terms of Meadow's expertise and professionalism provides a poignant example of the social construction of expert knowledge and the scientific principles on which it claims to be built. Relying on vague and speculative assertions – for example, 'in general there appears to be a one in two chance of similar or serious abuse occurring to a sibling of a child who has been smothered' (cited in *File on Four*, 8–9) – Meadow's credentials nevertheless ensured his status as one of the most eminent paediatricians in the world:

> He is Emeritus Professor of Paediatrics and Childcare . . . Bachelor of Medicine and Surgery, Fellow of the Royal College of Physicians, Fellow of the Royal College of Paediatric Child Health, with a diploma in obstetrics and gynaecology and a diploma in child health. He is past chairman of the most important groups in the field and was for eight years editor of the Archive of Disease in Childhood, a prestigious European journal, and the ABC of Child Abuse. His contribution to paediatrics was recognised by a knighthood in 1996. For twenty-five years he was a consultant at St James Hospital.
>
> (Batt 2004, 127)

Moreover, he was described as having 'great charm and charisma; he is avuncular . . . He is a clever witness, reluctant to condemn the mothers he accuses, which makes his testimony powerful' (Batt 2004, 127; Frith 2003, 8; Taylor 2003, 3). Such credentials and characteristics placed his testimony at the top of the truth-producing hierarchy of credibility within a culture where success in establishing official discourse and dominant truths 'comes from the respect of hierarchy, from reference to sacred texts and people, to being able to talk and give evidence using appropriate language and adopting proper postures and attitudes' as explained in Chapter 2 (Inglis 2003, 177; Carlen 1976). His claim to 'scientificity' ensured he had the authority to identify 'truths' and 'facts'. Moreover, the 'objectivity' and 'neutrality' associated with 'scientificity' ensured the power relationships wherein 'expert knowledge is generated was opaque and mystified' and as such, his success in establishing the dominant 'truth' about Sally provides a powerful example of Foucault's observation that 'far from preventing knowledge, power produces it' (in Gordon 1980, 59). For 20 years Meadow reigned as an eminent 'judge of normality', his theories and expert testimonies in court having gone unchallenged until the Sally Clark case (Baird, Parliamentary Debate 2004, 8; Taylor 2003, 3).

However, Inglis's reminder discussed in Chapter 2, that 'institutions and experts who claim to speak the truth should be treated with wariness and critical reflection' (2003, 3), also carried special significance for those who could not accept Sally's guilt, since the case also illustrates that even the most powerful truth producers can be challenged, for as critics began to question his methods and theories, his credibility unravelled. As noted above, in the first appeal the key point of contention regarding Meadow's evidence was his 1 in 73 million statistic. The extent of the invalidity and distortion of this statistic is reinforced by the fact that the President for the Royal Statistical Society wrote to the Lord Chancellor, 'expressing his extreme concern and calling for the courts to rethink the way they handle statistical evidence' (Hill 2005, 14; Royal Statistical Society 23 October 2001).[6] However, although his misleading and inaccurate statistic was to become the most notorious aspect of his evidence, it was by no means the only issue to cast doubt over whether his expertise matched his credentials.

First, when asked to comment on the fact that Harry died only five hours after his inoculation, Meadow claimed 'there is a slightly diminished chance of a baby dying within 48 hours, so completely discount immunisation as a cause of death' (cited in Batt 2004, 129). This is an unambiguous statement that, in its very certainty, suggests unawareness of the 1979 Vaccine Damage Payment Act, established 'to compensate children killed or harmed by vaccination' (Batt 2004, 131), which would not be in existence if there were a 'diminished chance' of a baby dying following vaccination.

Second, he claimed to have discovered that 81 cases, which had originally been classed as SIDS deaths, were in reality murder. Prior to the trial, Sally's defence team had repeatedly requested copies of the research on which Meadow's data were based, 'the request was denied. Professor Meadow claimed to have destroyed the majority of the information on which his published results were based' (SA 2003, 17; Batt 2004, 126). There was thus no opportunity for other scientists to check or verify his results. Professor Golding, herself a prosecution witness in the Angela Cannings case, called his methodology 'stamp-collecting':

> you pick out the cases you want to present and then you present them It was never a way of doing proper scientific research . . . he had no control group . . . he doesn't use the scientific rigour that I would respect . . . Should he give evidence in criminal trials? I'd rather he didn't.
>
> (cited in *File on Four* 2002, 4)

6 For further details please see Hill, who argued that the squaring of 8543 was invalid since 'the two deaths could not be deemed to be independent events'; and that Meadow was wrong to base his calculation on the whole birth rate in the UK per year, as the figures he used was only applicable to 'the much smaller sub-population having three special characteristics' (Hill 2005, 14).

Third, during his investigation into cases of other children whom Meadow, in contrast to other expert witnesses, had claimed died due to 'delayed effects of smothering', John Sweeney learned that one such child had improved in hospital, and that this improvement was measured as a matter of routine, 'using the Modified Glasgow Coma Score'. Not only was Meadow unable to explain this improvement – 'it is not normal, and it does not fit in with the other observations, it is a descripant and I cannot explain it' – he also appeared ignorant of the Modified Glasgow Coma Score:

> I'm not sure what she means by the Modified Glasgow Coma Scale, I am unfamiliar with using the scale on young children and it was certainly not the practice in our hospital . . . It sounds like a system that they have found helpful rather than an internationally or indeed scientifically standardised test.
>
> (cited in *File on Four* 2002, 8)

Upon further investigation Sweeney discovered that:

> The Modified Glasgow Coma Score is the standard test in children's wards in Britain and around the world and has been used at Sir Roy's old hospital, St James since 1996.
>
> (*File on Four* 2002, 8)

Sweeney invited Meadow to participate in his programme *File on Four* (2 July 2002), to explain this apparent ignorance of standard procedures not only in his own hospital, but throughout the entire UK and internationally – he declined.

The *File on Four* programme was not only concerned with Meadow's evidence in relation to children who had died, but also his appearances in the Family Court where his evidence would regularly result in children being removed from their homes and taken into care. For example, the Carter family had lost all four of their children as a result of Meadow once again straying outside his area of expertise and into that of toxology. On this occasion he claimed that between six and 12 imipramine tablets were needed for a child to be poisoned. As it was 'inconceivable' that an 18-month-old would swallow so many tablets voluntarily, he concluded her mother was suffering from MSbP and must have poisoned her child. Meadow produced no evidence to support his assertion, unlike toxicopathologist Dr Howard, who, in referring to 'the Paediatric Emergency Medicine Textbook',[7] was able to establish that only *one* tablet was needed to poison a young child. However, due to the Family Court's reliance on Meadow's testimony, the Carter family, and many others like them, had lost their children to foster parents (*File on Four* 2002, 5, 6). This was largely due to two factors: the Family Court requires a lower standard of proof than in Criminal Courts, and cases are regularly concluded after hearing uncontested evidence from only one expert. Prior to the

7 Fourth edition by Fleischer and Ludwig (*File on Four* 2002, 6).

Sally Clark case, Meadow had been 'a permanent professional witness',[8] particularly in cases 'where there was no direct or circumstantial evidence':

> He was called in to say, 'Now that I have looked at one of these parents' – almost invariably the mother – 'she resembles the type of person who does injure their child'. That was about the size of the evidence he gave.
>
> (Baird, Parliamentary Debate 2004, 4)

The legal system thus bestowed him with considerable, if hidden, power which had made him 'very arrogant' (Baird, Parliamentary Debate 2004, 8, 7). Legal personnel had been 'carried along' and 'blinded by evidence of experts such as Professor Meadow, without looking for corroborative evidence' (Osborne, Parliamentary Debate 2004, 3). Yet, the system itself had created this symbiotic environment between law and expert knowledge, since 'most of the judiciary have been taught by Professor Meadow that this is the right approach to sudden infant death, because he was the lecturer of choice at the Judicial Studies Board for a long time' (Baird, Parliamentary Debate 2004, 9). As observed by Batt, 'no wonder so many judges set great store by his opinions' (2004, 127).

Arguably, it was not only Meadow who had become arrogant, but also the judiciary itself, for despite the escalating controversy over his testimonies following the Clark and Cannings cases, he apparently still carried legitimacy in the eyes of the prosecution who did not hesitate to call upon his services again in 2003 when Trupti Patel was accused of murdering her children. That legitimacy was not replicated within the ranks of her jury who refused to convict (Sweeney 2003, 27). Up to that point, however, his long and intimate history with the judiciary serves as a poignant example of the myth of expert 'objectivity' and 'neutrality'. This myth was further reinforced by the chair of CCRC, Professor Graham Zellick, who in 2004 observed that although 'some so-called experts . . . were "highly dubious" and "appear to be making it up as they go along"' they were nevertheless handsomely rewarded for their efforts:

> Some people could make a good living from appearing as expert witnesses, and the more definitively their testimony supported the case, the more likely lawyers were to call on them again.
>
> (cited in Cowan 2004, 9)

Personal financial gain of this nature arguably stretches the credibility of 'value-free' and 'independent' expert knowledge to its very limit and instead suggests a close relationship between rates of conviction and profit-making by experts for hire.

The hidden, but very real power of expert knowledge was exemplified, not only in Meadow's relationship with the judiciary, but also through his association with the medical profession and the social services. Thus, 18 months after the jury

8 Particularly in cases where he felt MSbP – 'now highly questionable' – existed (Baird 2004, 6).

had rejected his evidence in the Patel case, and in the same year as the General Medical Council (GMC) found him guilty of 'gross professional misconduct' (see conclusion), he continued to enjoy both national and international platforms on which to publicise his 'expertise':

> Later this month he will lecture to a 1,500-strong audience of child-protection workers from 30 countries . . . in San Diego . . . 'The Quest for the Best' conference is billed as a platform for health workers to learn 'best practices'. Meadow is to give a lecture entitled 'the Medical Diagnosis of MSBP – Warning signs and Strategies for Diagnosis'. In a separate lecture he will also discuss how the backlash against MSBP has affected the paediatrics profession. When Meadow addressed British doctors last November, they were awarded 'personal development points' on their CVs for attending.
>
> (Doward 2005, 6)

In sum, an in-depth examination of the evidence of Meadow and Williams, the only two experts who had insisted Sally had killed her babies, reveals that neither was able to produce 'value-free', 'objective', 'scientific' evidence to support their claim. However, there is plenty of evidence of the child abuse caused by experts who repeatedly give testimonies that lead to parents losing their children to care or adoption, or separate children from their mothers by imprisoning innocent women. As observed by Sweeney, 'it is a form of child abuse for the state to jail a child's mother for no good reason' (2003, 27). Moreover, while innocent mothers were pursued through the courts during this modern witch-hunt, the cases of thousands of babies who died as a *direct consequence* of expert opinions have never been investigated:

> A major avoidable cause of cot death, was medical advice to mothers to put their babies to sleep face down – parroted by every doctor; midwife and health visitor. This resulted in a huge international increase in cot deaths, killing many thousands of babies throughout the developed world. How that erroneous policy – without supporting evidence – came about and spread so quickly has never been investigated and the story has been buried.
>
> (Lawrence Beech 2003, 17)

This example provides further evidence of the inequality between the institutional power of those who can claim scientific or legal status, and individuals such as Sally Clark who became a victim of both. It is also another powerful example of the myth of science's ability to uncover the 'truth' through value-free, objective methods. Instead it demonstrates 'the authority to identify "empirical truths" and to interpret observable, testable "facts" is dependent on existing power relations within given social contexts'" as argued above.

Agency, Gender and Expert Knowledge

In documenting the rise of expert knowledge, early feminist work identified the role it played in pathologising both women's bodies – particularly with regard to normal reproductive functions – and their minds, by denying or minimising female agency (Ehrenreich and English 1979; Showalter 1987; Ussher 1989; 1991). Relying on dominant social constructions of femininity which portray women as emotional, hysterical and irrational, and female criminals as mad, bad or a victim of circumstances – more sinned against than sinners – the threat that they present to the social order can be neutralised. In Allen's words, the denial of women's agency is a strategy for 'rendering them harmless' (1987b, 54). Thus, regardless of which of these labels are attached to female defendants, they all serve to insure that 'understanding of human female criminal agency . . . remains non-existent' (Morrissey 2003, 34).

As noted in Chapter 2, the challenge for feminism is therefore to succeed in acknowledging women's agency and accountability when they commit crime, without this leading to 'a concomitant increase in their liability for punishment' (Morrissey 2003, 68). This, however, has proved to be a difficult task, for as noted in relation to the Ellis appeal, while women's status has undeniably changed in recent decades to the point where formal equality between the sexes has been achieved – with these 'new types of freedom', new forms of oppression have also emerged (McNay 2004, 171). Moody notes that 'changes in the status of women may have had an impact on judicial attitudes' (1995, 223), and evidence of this can be observed in Sally's trial, where the very equality she represented – a highly educated, financially independent working lawyer – could be used against her to suggest a lack of maternal feelings. That very equality – which included working in a profession historically dominated by men – allowed her to become demonised as an unfit mother (Farrall 2009, 187). Thus, 'the first question put to her in cross-examination was, "You were not cut out to be a mother, were you?"' (cited in Kennedy 2005, 77). She was described as 'career-obsessed', and in his closing speech the prosecutor portrayed Sally 'as a baby-murderer whose motives for killing her babies were that she resented the interference with her career, she hated being fat and ugly and she couldn't get into her clothes' (Batt 2004, 198).

The strategy adopted by the prosecution in Sally's case thus confirms that 'the courtroom remains a gendered space which frequently functions as a key arena' for reinforcing traditional discourses of femininity, as argued in Chapter 5, for it is inconceivable that a man would be considered an unfit father as a result of being a successful lawyer. On the contrary, Sally's 'deviancy' lay in characteristics admired, expected or taken for granted in men – being professionally ambitious and having a taste for alcohol. Her very success, her lack of helplessness, her rejection of overly feminine attire for her court appearances and instead appearing in business suits, exemplified her failure to act according to traditional discourses of femininity and ensured she did not cut a sympathetic figure (Batt 2004, 97). Instead, 'she was repeatedly described as a career woman who had a luxury, dream-home, as though there was clearly no place for babies in her world'

(Kennedy 2005, 78). Meanwhile, as indicated above, the prosecution did not hesitate to emphasise the coroner's critique of her hope for another baby which thus stands as another example of 'doomed if you do doomed if you don't' in relation to discourses around motherhood.

Moreover, discourses of stereotypical gendered caricatures were activated via the numerous references to her husband's loyalty and gallantry – the suggestion being he had consistently lied to protect his manipulative, malignant wife (Batt 2004, 180; Ballinger 2000, 231). Thus, although his testimony provided strong supporting evidence of Sally's innocence, it was not taken seriously; instead, like Sally's own account, it became subjugated knowledge which could be dismissed in favour of the knowledge created by the 'rational procedures of law' and science (Ballinger 2005, 68).

In sum, Sally's failure to construct herself as the helpless, hapless victim associated with dominant femininity allowed a false agency to be manufactured during the complex interplay between expert knowledge and the legal process during her trial, which subsequently resulted in a conviction in a case where no crime had occurred. Thus, ironically, from a feminist perspective, while historically legal personnel and experts have dismissed women's agency by pathologising their behaviour, this process was reversed in the case of Sally Clark who was accredited with agency where none existed – the deliberate killing of two of her children. As such, her case represents a compelling example of 'equality with a vengeance'.

Re-Visiting the Processes behind Truth Production

The issues explored in relation to the Sally Clark case have exemplified many of the knowledge-generating processes outlined in Chapter 2, not least the way in which law and science play a key role in producing official discourse and securing the 'reproduction and perpetuation of patriarchal relations' due to the inherently phallocentric nature of both (Ballinger 2005, 68). In Foucauldian terms, it is this phallocentric framework that allows 'normality' and 'abnormality' to be interpreted through 'a regime of truth' that ensures definitions of these terms appear as commonsensical (Foucault in Gordon 1980, 133). In terms of law, the case-study has also demonstrated O'Donovan's observation that knowledge claims are made through phallocentric language such as '"the reasonable man" without any reliance on supporting evidence, empirical or evidentiary' because judges are 'ordained by state law to decide what is beyond reasonable doubt' (1993, 428). In turn, this confirms Inglis's point that the institutionalised hierarchies of legal procedures enable 'decisions of judges to appear as neutral and universally true' (Bourdieu in Inglis 2003, 172).

In terms of expert knowledge, Inglis's observations, as outlined in Chapter 2, that medical 'discourse in the legal field on sanity, madness and personality defects' (2003, 179) has become recognised as 'the truth', largely as a result of being able to refer to back to 'sacred text and people' and 'giving evidence using appropriate language and adopting proper postures and attitudes', are also evident (2003, 177).

It will be clear from the above examples of legal and scientific knowledge constructions that both have their foundations firmly rooted in the core principle of Enlightenment philosophy described earlier – 'that particular kinds of persons (trained, experts, scientists) have a greater degree of access to knowledge' about the 'true' nature of reality (Stanley and Wise 1993, 189). The Sally Clark case-study therefore also illustrates the very point at which this modernist approach to truth production generates subjugated knowledge, as well as the way in which that production is based on the disqualification of 'minor' knowledge such as that of Sally and Stephen Clark, 'in order to promote the centralisation, normalisation and disciplinarisation of dominant knowledges' (Foucault 2004, 288).

Finally the case-study has demonstrated the way in which the state contributes to the maintenance of modernist knowledge production – via the criminal justice system – by symbolically dominating 'over the means of producing and proclaiming the truth' as to whether someone's guilty, criminal, mad or poor (Inglis 2003, 176). As noted in Chapter 2, this process 'limits our ability to reflect critically about what really happened' (Inglis 2003, 6). Furthermore, even though defendants like Sally Clark are offered the opportunity to present their version of the truth to the court, that truth will nevertheless go through a process of mediation by legal personnel and expert witnesses to comply with the 'rational' procedures of law (Smart 1989, 9).

On the other hand, it is also important to reiterate that law and expert knowledge do not conspire to pursue innocent women through the courts. Indeed, the very fact that a second appeal quashed Sally's conviction demonstrates that law itself provides spaces within which it can be challenged, and thus, potentially turn subjugated knowledge into official discourse. Nonetheless, the symbiotic relationship between law and expert knowledge remained strong while Meadow could be relied upon to play his part in securing convictions. Only when the producers of subjugated knowledge – Stephen Clark, investigative journalists and the public, as represented in the Patel jury – shattered this legitimacy, did law distance itself from expert knowledge, and only after Trupti Patel's non-guilty verdict did Meadow disappear from the courtroom. In short, while the second appeal judges' willingness to challenge the ruling in the first appeal should not be underestimated, legal legitimacy was maintained by ignoring circumstantial evidence described in the first appeal as 'of the greatest significance'. Thus, the original verdict was reconstructed 'as an assessment of guilt that depended solely on the medical experts' . . . evidence':

> This in turn allowed them to deal with the safety of the convictions solely on the basis of the previously undisclosed evidence, and its interpretation by medical experts.
>
> (Nobles and Schiff 2004, 241)

In other words, 'having reduced the evidence of guilt solely to medical evidence, the Court was able to presume that the previous Court, would, had it known of the non-disclosed test results, never have concluded that the evidence pointed overwhelmingly to guilt' (Nobles and Schiff 2004, 241). As discussed earlier in relation to the Ruth Ellis appeal, when these legal manoeuvres are observed 'law's power to define and disqualify . . . [and] its ability to redefine the truth of events' becomes visible (Smart 1989, 164). In that sense it is vital that feminism is not seduced by law's eventual recognition of Sally's innocence, for it can be understood to have merely remedied a problem it itself had created, a process which ultimately restored its legitimacy, and arguably, increased its own power 'by confirming that it is the most appropriate body to' establish the 'truth' (Ballinger 2012, 20). It is thus the power of law itself – together with its symbiotic relationship with expert knowledge, which should be challenged – for without a de-centring of both, their 'superior position at the apex of the hierarchy of truth production will be maintained' (Ballinger 2012, 20). Foucault has observed:

> The essential political problem for the intellectual is not to criticise the ideological contents supposedly linked to science, or to ensure that his own scientific practice is accompanied by a correct ideology, but that of ascertaining the possibility of constituting a new politics of truth. The problem is not changing people's consciousnesses – or what's in their heads – but the political, economic, institutional regime of the production of truth.
>
> (Foucault in Gordon 1980, 132, 133)

The Sally Clark case has demonstrated that this is as true for law as it is for science.

Conclusion

> These everyday discourses of truth that kill . . . are at the very heart of our judicial system.
>
> (Foucault 2003, 6)

Sally and Stephen Clark had been educated to a high level and, as lawyers, both worked in one aspect of the legal system. Moreover, as a retired Divisional Commander and Chief of the Police, Sally's father, Frank Lockyer, had considerable experience and understanding of the operations of the criminal justice system. Their tireless search for evidence, which would eventually attract the attention of CCRC, is arguably the key, if not the only reason behind Sally's release. Yet, there is evidence indicating that the incompetence displayed by Dr Williams, as articulated by the second appeal judges, is not an isolated case. For example, following the death of Ian Tomlinson in 2009, after he was captured on camera being struck by the truncheon of a police officer, Home Office pathologist Freddy Patel carried out Tomlinson's post-mortem, and concluded he had died of cardiac arrest. A second post-mortem revealed he had in fact died of 'internal injuries', and following a Medical Practitioners Tribunal investigation, it emerged Mr Patel had made several other errors (BBC News 6 September 2012). Other examples include that of Dr Michael Heath who 'resigned from the Home Office' in 2006, after his work was exposed as being 'based on an "unacceptable level of speculation"' (Laville 2006, 14).

The cases of Drs Williams, Patel and Heath have come to the attention of the media. What cannot be known is how many other alternative truths are being suppressed, how many other defendants' or victims' knowledges have become subjugated through incompetent or inaccurate expert knowledge being uncritically accepted by a judiciary over-familiar with, and over-reliant on, a stock set of experts able to enhance their status through impressive lists of qualifications. Furthermore, in the wake of the Clark, Cannings and Patel cases, the Royal College of Pathologists commissioned the *Sudden Unexpected Death in Infancy Report* (SUDI) which recommended that *more* experts were needed 'to boost a failing system' (Boseley and Dyer 2004, 6). This recommendation arguably has the potential to *increase and strengthen* the influence of expert knowledge.

The Sally Clark case was open to public and media scrutiny. No such scrutiny exists in the Family Court Division which takes place in private and lower standards of proof are accepted. Professor Meadow acted as the sole witness in numerous such cases, and on his say-so the lives of hundreds of families have been destroyed as a result of children being taken into care or adopted after he claimed they had been abused. These families represent a 'cacophony of silence' – voices forever subjugated – as it was decided by politicians that the children's interests would be best served by remaining with their adoptive or foster parents. Sally and Stephen Clark themselves experienced this additional injustice, when their youngest child was placed with a foster family during the first year of his life.[9]

Following Sally's acquittal, a review of 49 cases affected by Dr Williams's work took place (Campbell and Walker undated, 27–8). Following a tribunal in December 2005, Dr Williams lost his accreditation to carry out post-mortems for the Home Office for a period of three years (Dyer 2005, 10). However, an Appeal Panel reinstated him in 2007 'on the basis that he had made an honest albeit serious error, which was not likely to be repeated and which he had not sought to conceal' (Campbell and Walker undated, 32).

When the unreliability of Professor Meadow's theories and testimonies was finally exposed, the 'Attorney-General announced an immediate review of 258 criminal cases which had concluded with "guilty" verdicts and which could potentially prove to be miscarriages of justice as a result of Meadow's expert testimony' (Osborne, Parliamentary Debate 2004, 1).

Having been struck off the medical register after being found guilty of 'serious professional misconduct' by the General Medical Council in 2005, Professor Meadow regained his licence in 2006 after Mr Justice Collins overruled the Council's decision. Justifying his ruling the judge offered these insights:

> This case was presented by the media as Prof Meadow's evidence having caused a miscarriage of justice. That's unfair, manifestly unfair . . . It may have contributed to it – who knows? – but the suggestion that it caused it is wrong and always has been.
>
> (*Guardian* 18 February 2006)

9 Stephen Clark eventually gained custody of the couple's remaining son.

The symbiotic relationship between law and expert knowledge had thus been successfully restored. The heavy price for these experts' wrong-doing was to be paid elsewhere, for as the victim of their misconduct, Sally Clark, was not to enjoy the privilege of such an unproblematic return to her former existence. She died in 2007, aged 42. She had endured severe post-traumatic stress disorder and 'protracted grief reaction' during the four years after her release, and 'never fully recovered from the effects of this appalling miscarriage of justice' (BBC News UK 22 November 2007). It is hardly surprising that when a Home Office pathologist carried out her post-mortem, Sally's family instructed a second pathologist to attend the examination 'so they could have confidence in the results' (Glendinning 2007, 11).

7 Conclusion

The contents of this book can be summarised under three inter-related themes: a history of the present, a history from below and continuity and change. First, in terms of a history of the present, while the case-studies included in this book provide valuable examples of history-writing being able to make 'the already-dead . . . speak and walk amongst us' (Steedman 2014, 162), such knowledge from the past can also be utilised 'to disturb contemporary conceptions and help bring about change' (Garland 2014, 371). In that sense this book has sought to follow Roth's definition of what it means to write this particular type of history: 'Writing a history *of* the present means writing history *in* the present; self-consciously writing in a field of power relations and political struggle' (Roth cited in Garland 2014, 373, original emphasis).

In so doing, it has also aimed to incorporate an analysis of what Foucault has termed 'phenomena of the past' for he was convinced that such phenomena have a profound impact on the present, as he explained in an interview with Simon:

> I was interested in them – in fact profoundly interested – because I saw in them ways of thinking and behaving that are still with us. I try to show, based upon their historical establishment and formation, those systems that are still ours today, and within which we are trapped. It is a question, basically, of presenting a critique of our own time based upon retrospective analyses.
>
> (Foucault in Simon 1971, 192; see also Garland 2014, 371)

In this book 'phenomena of the past' have been those processes, policies and practices built around gender, power and punishment as well as the subsequent 'truths' which spring from the didactical relationship between them. The analysis presented in Chapter 5 is particularly relevant and poignant in relation to Foucault's emphasis on the importance of past phenomena because 'the ways of thinking and behaving that are still with us' were made visible nearly half a century after the trial of Ruth Ellis had taken place, in the form of her appeal in 2003. When considering its outcome, it would indeed appear to be the case that we are still trapped within historical formations and systems in relation to gender and punishment, as well as the often sexist and misogynous perceptions of female defendants, institutionalised within the state, and more broadly, in popular culture. This point was reiterated and emphasised in Chapter 6 through the analysis of the Sally Clark case, which indicated that a failure to comply adequately and obsequiously with traditional discourses of motherhood and domesticity remain important legal tools which are mobilised to discredit female defendants up to, and into, the twenty-first century. Thus, the aim of this book has been, not only to document a historical context to gendered state responses where contemporary female defendants are concerned, but also to utilise that historical context 'as a means of critical engagement with the present' as advocated by Foucault (Garland 2014, 367). In doing so, the book challenges the dominant, benevolent view of 'progress' that is frequently associated with debates around gender equality and the law, for as Weedon notes, legal equality 'has not proved any great threat to the balance of power in a society where patriarchal relations inform the very production and regulation of female and male subjects' (cited in Smart 1989, 88).

A History from Below

In terms of a 'history from below' (Arnot 2002, 149), or, in Foucauldian terms, 'subjugated knowledges' (2004, 7), a constant theme throughout this book has been the status of knowledge – the focus being on the difference between those who have the power to establish the 'truth' through the dissemination of official discourses, and those who are disempowered and silenced in that process. Thus, in the *Introduction* the importance of deconstructing 'the truth' arrived at, following the conclusion of the criminal trial, was discussed and emphasised. Throughout the remaining chapters this issue has been explored in a number of different historical contexts. Chapter 3 outlined the processes through which official state truths presided over what was in effect an unsafe conviction. If one was granted the ability to momentarily ignore the status of who was speaking in the Louie Calvert case – Louie or state servants – who appears to have constructed the most plausible and the most credible narrative in relation to the death of Lily Waterhouse?

Conversely, Chapter 4 sought to challenge a fundamental aspect of how the punishment of women is understood through the dominant discourses of the leniency versus harshness debate. The chapter documented the way in which 'knowledge from below' – far from being ignored by state servants – was in fact considered an important factor, when it came to maintaining legitimacy for the criminal justice system and its response to the gender-specific crime of infanticide.

Finally, Chapter 6 aimed to illustrate the excessive power contained within official discourse that was forged by the union of two truth-producing bodies located at the top of the 'hierarchy of credibility' (Becker 1967) – those of law and expert knowledge. Such was the power of the dominant discourses surrounding the Clark case that two murders were invented – an invention that led directly to a miscarriage of justice – and indirectly, to the untimely death of the real victim of this case – Sally Clark herself.

Continuity and Change

> Material feminists tend to offer . . . cautious accounts of change asserting that, if gender relations are transforming at all . . . it is in a gradual and complex fashion where the emergence of new forms of autonomy coincides with new forms of dependency and subordination.
>
> (McNay 2004, 174)

In terms of the third theme, continuity and change, this book has sought to illustrate the continued existence of the chasm between the success in achieving formal gender equality, and the failure to put this into practice in order to also achieve substantive equality for women. In the words of Fraser, 'second-wave feminism has wrought an epochal cultural revolution, but the vast change in *mentalities* has not (yet) translated into structural, institutional change' (2013, 210, original emphasis). McRobbie has explained the persistence of this chasm between formal and substantial equality thus:

> The kind of feminism which is taken into account . . . is liberal, equal opportunities feminism . . . what is invoked more negatively is the radical feminism concerned with social criticism rather than with progress or improvement in the position of women in an otherwise more or less unaltered social order.
>
> (2009, 14)

McRobbie elaborates by pointing to the consistent 'displacement of feminism as a political movement' through the postmodern discourse of feminist concerns having 'already been taken into account', as explained in Chapter 2. She describes this 'already taken into accountness' as resulting in an 'overturning of feminist gains, a resurgent patriarchal attempt to undo the achievements of the women's movement in the spheres of work and home' (2009, 48). The processes involved in the construction of the postmodern 'already taken into accountness' appear to be 'inevitable' and 'seem to free up people . . . giving them more choices', yet they 'are in fact new and more complex ways of ensuring that masculine domination is re-instated, and at the same time protected from the possibility of a new feminism' (2009, 48). In short: 'Women are currently being disempowered through the very discourses of empowerment they are being offered as substitutes for feminism' (McRobbie 2009, 49).

McRobbie's analysis can thus be seen to link directly to another persistent theme of this book – the extraordinary capacity of dominant heteropatriarchal discourses to re-group and re-invent themselves into new forms of oppression. This is further exacerbated by the postmodern emphasis on 'difference', which has resulted in a measure of fragmentation within the feminist critique of official state-sanctioned discourses, from which it has never recovered. Instead, in terms of continuity and change, an uneasy and unresolved relationship between progress in women's formal equality and the archaic, yet contemporary procedures within law and court proceedings remain, as demonstrated in Chapter 5.

Overall, it becomes clear that the state has not remained impervious to the critiques of second-wave feminists, on the contrary, it can be seen to have actively engaged with some of the issues raised by them, for example with respect to violence against women and children. Yet, it is equally clear that such issues have been selectively incorporated into the mainstream *without* paying attention to the wider, structural vision of social justice formulated by the feminist critique, and without adequately considering the gender specific nature of male violence arising out of the interpersonal and wider politics of masculinity.

In this way, as argued in Chapter 5, official state power has been able to 'taketh' away with one hand what it has 'giveth' with the other. This form of recuperation of ground gained in order to defend the heteropatriarchal social order, and thus the status quo itself, cannot be adequately explained or understood without placing the state's role at the forefront of a gendered analysis. For this reason the book has emphasised the enduring validity and relevance of Connell's theory of hegemonic masculinity and its crucial role in 'doing gender', as outlined in Chapter 2. Here it was argued that Connell understands the state 'as an active player in gender politics' and 'at the very least a significant vehicle of sexual and gender oppression and regulation' (1994, 147). At the same time he argues against a patriarchal conspiracy by stressing that this oppression and regulation takes an indirect form due to being 'embedded in procedure' and 'objective' structures. It will be recalled from Chapter 2 that Connell utilises the example of rape to illustrate the operations involved when the state, via the criminal justice system, is 'doing gender'. In particular, he draws attention to the legal system's ability to translate interested points of view into 'procedural norms' that define 'what must be proven and what is acceptable evidence'. Connell thereby illustrates how the structure of law is patriarchal rather than 'biased against women', which, in turn, allows him to argue that the more objective these procedural norms are, 'the more effectively patriarchal they are'. In this way, 'the norm of "legal objectivity" . . . becomes an institutionalisation of men's interests' (1994, 145).

Here Connell demonstrates his support, first, for the feminist critique of 'objectivity' – that this is in fact a deeply androcentric concept, as documented in Chapter 2; and second, for the feminist argument, that law is both androcentric and patriarchal in nature. Once again, in relation to continuity and change, this does not mean that nothing has changed with regard to gender and punishment. Clearly it has, as discussed in Chapter 5 for example, in relation to the 2010 changes to the law (*Coroners and Justice Act 2009*; *Ministry of Justice Circular 2010/13*), regarding survivors of domestic violence who retaliate against their abusers. On the other hand, such changes – and indeed other reforms such as the *Sexual Offences Act* of 2003 – have done little, if anything, to radically change 'the wider social relationships and material realities which condition men's sexual violence and women's sexual victimisation. In short, the power of law remains unchallenged, as does the social context that makes sexual violation routine' (Phoenix and Oerton 2005, 39). A short case-study that took place exactly a century after Florence Boxhall stood trial (see Chapter 4), illustrates the continuing validity of Phoenix and Oerton's claim:

In November 2010 a woman was released from prison after having her eight-month sentence overturned for making a false complaint of rape. The release was prompted by the judge accepting that the woman 'had been the victim of prolonged domestic abuse and had been put under pressure by her husband to withdraw the allegations' of anal, vaginal and oral rape (*Guardian* 24 November 2010). At no point had the woman claimed that her complaint was false. Instead, she stated that it was the retraction of the complaint, rather than the allegation that was false. Thus, her sentence was reduced to 'a community sentence with a two-year supervision order', due to her crime being that of 'falsely retracting a truthful allegation' rather than having made a false complaint of rape (*Guardian* 24 November 2010). In short, as a direct consequence of having made a truthful complaint of rape this woman had acquired a criminal record. That was the truth in November 2010, although one year earlier the truth had been that she had made a false accusation of rape.

This case provides one example of the persistence of key issues and themes identified in this book into the twenty-first century. First, it is noted that the initial 'truth' about the case as constructed by the legal system, was in fact false. Second, a space existed on which subjugated knowledge could challenge this official discourse and the woman's voice was eventually allowed to be heard and her version of the truth was accepted. Third, despite this acceptance, 'the appeal judges nevertheless ruled that the "appropriate" sentence was a community sentence with a two-year supervision order' as noted above ' . . . while her husband walked free' (*Guardian* 24 November 2010). In the words of one observer: 'How come a victim of domestic violence and rape is the one with a two-year community sentence and a criminal record?' (Professor McGlynn cited in *Guardian* 24 November 2010).

This case also reiterates the ongoing existence of specific continuities in relation to the criminal justice system's response to women – defendants or victims – which span an entire century. For example, the state's response to the crime of infanticide in the first decade of the twentieth century, and the twenty-first century response to the crime of rape, have taken a particular form: to emphasise the *individual* suffering of *individual deserving* – yet still punishable – victims/criminals whose circumstances were such that they must be taken into account by a sympathetic, but overwhelmingly, patriarchal legal system. That 'taken into accountness' ensures that no structural changes are required which could, potentially, have addressed women's subordinate position within a heteropatriarchal social order. The state can thus be understood as having 'done gender' by undermining feminist discourses which had identified the criminal justice system itself as the problem, rather than the solution.

In sum, the solution to the type of crimes identified in the case-studies in this book – infanticide/child killing by abandoned, destitute women, a retaliating victim who killed her abuser, an, arguably, manslaughter/accidental killing, leading to an unsafe conviction, and an eventual undisputed miscarriage of justice – cannot be found within the law, since these trials were overwhelmingly exercises in gendered power relationships. They were all exercised 'in the masculine mode, so one is not the solution to the other' (Smart 1989, 88). To reiterate another recurring theme of this book: 'the state is not an objective, neutral arbiter of the "facts"' (Walklate 2007, 49). Instead it has gender deeply embedded within it, and as such, its self-maintenance includes activities which encourage the production and reproduction of the gendered subject which, in turn, support the existing social order (Smart 1995, 79). The criminal justice system and the law itself, provide crucial contributions towards this production and reproduction, law reform cannot therefore be the answer to gender injustice. Smart notes the importance of resisting 'the temptation that law offers, namely the promise of a solution' (1989, 164). Yet, she also emphasises the importance of the legal forum as a site of struggle, where feminist re-definitions of events can challenge the power of law to define and disqualify – at the point where 'law asserts its definition, feminism can assert its alternative' (1989, 165). Without such re-definitions of female defendants' lived experiences and motivations law's superior position at the apex of the hierarchy of truth production will be maintained and the continuity of 'hidden silencing' (Mathiesen 2004) assured, not only in relation to the Ellis case discussed above, but in relation to all the case-studies documented in this book. Feminism is therefore facing an ongoing struggle to establish women's way of knowing generally, and feminist knowledge specifically, as legitimate knowledge inside and outside the courtroom, in order to provide a direct challenge to the established 'order of things'[1] – the heteropatriarchal social order.

1 This phrase is borrowed from the title of Foucault's *The Order of Things: An Archaeology of the Human Sciences* (1977).

References

Allen, H. (1987a) *Justice Unbalanced* Milton Keynes: Open University Press.

Allen, H. (1987b) 'Rendering Them Harmless: The Professional Portrayal of Women Charged with Serious Violent Crimes' in Carlen, P. and Worrall, A. (eds) *Gender, Crime and Justice* Milton Keynes: Open University Press.

Arnot, M.L. (2000) 'Understanding Women Committing Newborn Child Murder in Victorian England' in D'Cruze, S. (ed.) *Everyday Violence in Britain 1850–1950* London: Longman.

Arnot, M.L. (2002) 'The Murder of Thomas Sandles: Meanings of a Mid-Nineteenth-Century Infanticide' in Jackson, M. (ed.) *Infanticide: Historical Perspectives on Child Murder and Concealment, 1550–2000* Aldershot: Ashgate.

Ballinger, A. (1996) 'The Guilt of the Innocent and the Innocence of the Guilty' in Myers, A. and Wight, S. (eds) *No Angels* London: Pandora.

Ballinger, A. (2000) *Dead Woman Walking* Aldershot: Ashgate.

Ballinger, A. (2003) 'Researching and Redefining State Crime: Feminism and the Capital Punishment of Women' in Tombs, S. and Whyte, D. (eds) *Unmasking the Crimes of the Powerful* New York: Peter Lang.

Ballinger, A. (2005) 'Reasonable Women Who Kill: Re-Interpreting and Re-Defining Women's Response to Domestic Violence in England and Wales 1900–1965' *Outlines: Critical Social Studies* 7(2), 65–82.

Ballinger, A. (2007) 'Masculinity in the Dock: Legal Responses to Male Violence and Female Retaliation in England and Wales 1900–1965' *Social & Legal Studies* 16(4), 459–81.

Ballinger, A. (2008) 'Reconceptualising Social Control: A Case-Study in Gender, Punishment and Murder' in Johnson, H. (ed.) *Punishment and Control in Historical Perspective* Basingstoke: Palgrave.

Ballinger, A. (2009) 'Same as It Ever Was?' in Coleman, R., Sim, J., Tombs, S. and Whyte, D. (eds) *State, Power, Crime* London: Sage.

Ballinger, A. (2011) 'Feminist Research, State Power and Executed Women: The Case of Louie Calvert' in Farrell, S., Hough, M., Maruna, S. and Sparks, R. (eds) *Escape Routes: Contemporary Perspectives on Life after Punishment* Abingdon: GlassHouse.

Ballinger, A. (2012) 'A Muted Voice from the Past: The "Silent Silencing" of Ruth Ellis' *Social & Legal Studies* 21(4), 445–67.

Barnett, H. (1998) *Introduction to Feminist Jurisprudence* London: Cavendish.

Barstow, L.A. (1994) *Witchcraze* London: Pandora.

Batt, J. (2004) *Stolen Innocence* London: Ebury Press.

Becker, H. (1967) 'Whose Side Are We On?' *Social Problems* 14(3), 239–47.

Box, S. (1983) *Power, Crime and Mystification* London: Tavistock.

Brown, A. and Clare, E. (2005) 'A History of Experience: Exploring Prisoners' Accounts of Incarceration' in Emsley, C. (ed.) *The Persistent Prison: Problems, Images and Alternatives* London: Frances Boutle.

Burton, F. and Carlen, P. (1979) *Official Discourse: On Discourse, Analysis, Government Publications, Ideology and the State* London: Routledge & Kegan Paul.

Burton, M. (2001) 'Intimate Homicide and the Provocation Defence – Endangering Women? R. v Smith' *Feminist Legal Studies* 9, 247–58.

Burton, M. (2003) 'Sentencing Domestic Homicide upon Provocation: Still "Getting Away with Murder"' *Feminist Legal Studies* 11, 279–89.

Burton, M. (2010) 'The Legal Construction of Domestic Violence' in Jones, J., Grear, A., Fenton, R.A. and Stevenson, K. (eds) *Gender, Sexuality and Law* London: Routledge.

Cain, M. (1990a) 'Realist Philosophy and Standpoint Epistemologies or Feminist Criminology as a Successor Science' in Gelsthorpe, L. and Morris, A. (eds) *Feminist Perspectives in Criminology* Milton Keynes: Open University Press.

Cain, M. (1990b) 'Towards Transgression: New Directions in Feminist Criminology' *International Journal of the Sociology of Law* 18, 1–18.

Cain, M. (1993) 'Foucault, Feminism and Feeling: What Foucault Can and Cannot Contribute to Feminist Epistemology' in Ramazanoglu, C. (ed.) *Up Against Foucault* London: Routledge.

Calvert, L. (1926) *My Life Story* in HO144/6012.

Cannings, A. (2006) *Against All Odds: A Mother's Fight to Prove Her Innocence* London: Time Warner Books.

Carlen, P. (1976) *Magistrates' Justice* London: Martin Robertson.

Carlen, P. (1983) *Women's Imprisonment* London: Routledge & Kegan Paul.

Carlen, P. (1988) *Women, Crime and Poverty* Milton Keynes: Open University Press.

Carlen, P. (2002) *Women and Punishment* Cullompton: Willan Publishing.

Carline, A. (2005a) 'Women Who Kill their Abusive Partners: From Sameness to Gender Construction' *Liverpool Law Review* 26, 13–44.

Carline, A. (2005b) 'Zoora Shah: "An Unusual Woman"' *Social & Legal Studies* 14(2), 215–38.

Carrington, K. (2002) 'Feminism and Critical Criminology: Confronting Genealogies' in Carrington, K. and Hogg, R. (eds) *Critical Criminology* Cullompton: Willan.

Chan, W. (2001) *Women, Murder and Justice* Basingstoke: Palgrave.

Clark, A. (2000) 'Domesticity and the Problem of Wife-Beating in Nineteenth Century Britain: Working-Class Culture, Law and Politics' in D'Cruze, S. (ed.) *Everyday Violence in Britain 1850–1950* Harlow: Longman.

Collier, R. (1992) 'The Art of Living the Married Life: Representations of Male Heterosexuality in Law' *Social & Legal Studies* 1, 543–63.

Collier, R. (1995a) *Masculinity, Law and the Family* London: Routledge.

Collier, R. (1995b) 'A Father's "Normal" Love? Masculinities, Criminology and the Family' in Dobash, R. and Dobash, R. (eds) *Gender & Crime* London: Sage.

Comack, E. (1999) 'Producing Feminist Knowledge: Lessons from Women in Trouble' *Theoretical Criminology* 3(3), 287–306.

Conlon, G. (1990) *Proved Innocent* London: Hamish Hamilton.

Connell, R.W. (1987) *Gender & Power* Cambridge: Polity Press.

Connell, R.W. (1994) 'The State, Gender and Sexual Politics: Theory and Appraisal' in Radke, H.L. and Stam, H.J. (eds) *Power/Gender* London: Sage.

Criminal Law Policy Unit: *Ministry of Justice Circular 2010/13.*

Davies, M. (1997) 'Taking the Inside Out: Sex and Gender in the Legal Subject' in Naffine, N. and Owens, R.J. (eds) *Sexing the Subject of Law* London: Sweet & Maxwell Ltd.

Davies, M. (2007) 'Beyond Unity' in Munro, V.E. and Stychin, C.F. (eds) *Sexuality and the Law* Abingdon: Routledge/Cavendish.

Davis, A. (2001) 'Writing on the Wall: Prisoners on Punishment' *Punishment and Society* 3(3) 427–31.

Davis, K. (2008) 'Intersectionality as Buzzword: A Sociology of Science Perspective on What Makes a Feminist Theory Successful' *Feminist Theory* 9(1), 67–85.

Deveaux, M. (1994) 'Feminism and Empowerment: A Critical Reading of Foucault' *Feminist Studies* 20(2), 223–47.

Di Stefano, C. (1990) 'Dilemmas of Difference: Feminism, Modernity and Postmodernism' in Nicholson, L.J. (ed.) *Feminism/Postmodernism* London: Routledge.

Downing, L. (2013) *The Subject of Murder: Gender, Exceptionality and the Modern Killer* Chicago: University of Chicago Press.

Edwards, S. (1987) '"Provoking Her Own Demise": From Common Assault to Homicide' in Hanmer, J. and Maynard, M. (eds) *Women, Violence and Social Control* London: Macmillan.

Edwards, S. (1996) *Sex and Gender in the Legal Process* London: Blackstone Press.

Edwards, S. (2010) 'Anger and Fear as Justifiable Preludes for Loss of Self-Control' *Journal of Criminal Law* 74(3), 223–41.

Ehrenreich, B. and English, D. (1979) *For Her Own Good* London: Pluto.

Faith, K. (1993) *Unruly Women* Vancouver: Press Gang Publishers.

Farrall, S. (2009) '"We Just Live Day-to-Day": A Case Study of Life after Release Following Wrongful Conviction' in Lippens, R. and Crewe, D. (eds) *Existentialist Criminology* London: Routledge-Cavendish.

Farrall, S., Hough, M., Maruna, S. and Sparks, R. (eds) (2011) *Escape Routes: Contemporary Perspectives on Life After Punishment* Abingdon: GlassHouse.

Finch, E. and Munro, V. (2007) 'The Demon Drink and the Demonized Woman: Socio-Sexual Stereotypes and Responsibility Attribution in Rape Trials Involving Intoxicants' *Social & Legal Studies* 16(4), 591–614.

Fitz-Gibbon, K. and Pickering, S. (2012) 'Homicide Law Reform in Victoria, Australia' *British Journal of Criminology* 52, 159–80.

FitzRoy, L. (2001) 'Violent Women: Questions for Feminist Theory, Practice and Policy' *Critical Social Policy* 21(1), 7–34.

Flax, J. (1990) 'Postmodernism and Gender Relations in Feminist Theory' in Nicholson, L.N. (ed.) *Feminism/Postmodernism* London: Routledge.

Foucault, M. (1977) *Discipline and Punish* Harmondsworth: Peregrine Books.

Foucault, M. (1980) in Gordon, C. (ed.) *Power/Knowledge Selected Interviews and Other Writings 1972–1977* London: Harvester Wheatsheaf.

Foucault, M. (2003) *Abnormal: Lectures at the College De France 1974–1975* London: Verso.

Foucault, M. (2004) 'Society Must Be Defended' in Bertani, B. and Fontana, A. (eds) *Michel Foucault* London: Penguin Books.

Fox, M. (1995) 'Legal Responses to Battered Women Who Kill' in Bridgeman, J. and Millns, S. (eds) *Law and Body Politics* Aldershot: Dartmouth.

Fox, M. (2000) 'Feminist Perspectives on Theories of Punishment' in Nicolson, D. and Bibbings, L. (eds) *Feminist Perspectives on Criminal Law* London: Cavendish.

Franzway, S., Court, D. and Connell, R.W. (1989) *Staking a Claim: Feminism, Bureaucracy and the State* London: Allen & Unwin.

Fraser, N. (2013) *Fortunes of Feminism: From State-Managed Capitalism to Neoliberal Crisis* London: Verso.

Fraser, N. and Nicholson, L.J. (1990) 'Introduction' in Nicholson, L.J. (ed.) *Feminism/ Postmodernism* London: Routledge.

Frost, G. (2004) '"She Is but a Woman": Kitty Byron and the English Edwardian Criminal Justice System' *Gender and History* 16(3), 538–60.

Garland, D. (2014) 'What is a "History of the Present"? On Foucault's Genealogies and their Critical Preconditions' *Punishment & Society* 16(4), 365–84.

Gilligan, G. (2004) 'Official Inquiry, Truth and Criminal Justice' in Gilligan, G. and Pratt, J. (eds) *Crime, Truth and Justice: Official Inquiry, Discourse, Knowledge* Cullompton: Willan.

Gilligan, G. and Pratt, J. (eds) (2004) *Crime, Truth and Justice: Official Inquiry, Discourse, Knowledge* Cullompton: Willan.

Goodman, J. and Pringle, P. (1974) *The Trial of Ruth Ellis* London: David and Charles.

Gordon, C. (ed.) (1980) *Power/Knowledge: Selected Interviews and Other Writings 1972–1977* London: Harvester Wheatsheaf.

Hammerton, J. (1992) *Cruelty and Companionship: Conflict in Nineteenth Century Married Life* London: Routledge.

Hancock, R. (1989) *Ruth Ellis* London: Weidenfeld.

Harding, S. (1987) 'Introduction: Is there a Feminist Method?' and 'Conclusion: Epistemological Questions' in Harding, S. (ed.) *Feminism & Methodology* Milton Keynes: Open University Press.

Harding, S. (1990) 'Feminism, Science, and the Anti-Enlightenment Critiques' in Nicholson, L.J. (ed.) *Feminism/Postmodernism* London: Routledge.

Harding, S. (1996) 'Feminism, Science and the Anti-Enlightenment Critiques' in Garry, A. and Pearsall, M. (eds) *Women, Knowledge and Reality* London: Routledge.

Hay, D. (1977) 'Property, Authority and Criminal Law' in Hay, D., Linebaugh, P., Rule, J., Thompson, E.P. and Winslow, C. *Albion's Fatal Tree* Harmondsworth: Peregrine.

Haywood, C. and Mac an Ghaill, M. (1996) 'Schooling Masculinities' in Mac an Ghaill, M. (ed.) *Understanding Masculinities* Milton Keynes: Open University Press.

Haywood, C. and Mac an Ghaill, M. (2003) *Men and Masculinities* Buckingham: Open University Press.

Hearn, J. (1996) 'Is Masculinity Dead? A Critique of the Concept of Masculinity/ Masculinities' in Mac an Ghaill, M. (ed.) *Understanding Masculinities* Milton Keynes: Open University Press.

Heidensohn, F. (1986) *Women & Crime* Basingstoke: Macmillan.

Hester, M. (1998) 'Patriarchal Reconstruction and Witch Hunting' in Barry, J., Hester, M. and Roberts, G. (eds) *Witchcraft in Early Modern Europe: Studies in Culture and Belief* Cambridge: Past & Present Publications Cambridge University Press.

Hester, M. (1992) *Lewd Women & Wicked Witches* London: Routledge.

Higginbotham, A.R. (1992) '"Sin of the Age": Infanticide and Illegitimacy in Victorian London' in Garrigan, K.O. (ed.) *Victorian Scandals* Ohio: Ohio University Press.

Holmwood, J. (1995) 'Feminism and Epistemology: What Kind of Successor Science?' *Sociology* 29(3), 411–28.

Huggett, R. and Berry, P. (1956) *Daughters of Cain* London: Allen & Unwin Ltd.

Hunter, R. and Mack, K. (1997) 'Exclusion and Silence: Procedure and Evidence' in Naffine, N. and Owens, R.J. (eds) *Sexing the Subject of Law* London: Sweet & Maxwell Ltd.

Hutter, B. and Williams, G. (1981) *Controlling Women* London: Croom Helm.

Inglis, T. (2003) *Truth, Power and Lies* Dublin: University College Dublin Press.

Jackson, M. (1994) 'Suspicious Infant Deaths: The Statute of 1624 and Medical Evidence at Coroners' Inquests' in Clark, M. and Crawford, C. (eds) *Legal Medicine in History* Cambridge: Cambridge University Press.

Jackson, M. (2002) 'The Trial of Harriet Vooght: Continuity and Change in the History of Infanticide' in Jackson, M. (ed.) *Infanticide: Historical Perspectives on Child Murder and Concealment 1550–2000* Aldershot: Ashgate.

Kennedy, H. (1993) *Eve Was Framed* London: Vintage Books.

Kennedy, H. (2005) *Eve Was Framed*, 2nd edn London: Vintage Books.

Kilday, A.M. (2013) *A History of Infanticide in Britain c.1600 to the Present* Basingstoke: Palgrave Macmillan.

Klein, D. (1973) 'The Etology of Female Crime' in Muncie, J., McLaughlin, E. and Langan, M. (eds) (1996) *Criminological Perspectives* Sage: London.

Knelman, J. (1998) *Twisting in the Wind* Toronto: University of Toronto Press.

Kramar, K.J. and Watson, W.D. (2006) 'The Insanities of Reproduction: Medico-Legal Knowledge and the Development of Infanticide Law' *Social & Legal Studies* 15(2), 237–55.

Lacey, N. (2000) 'General Principles of Criminal Law? A Feminist View' in Nicolson, D. and Bibbings, L. (eds) *Feminist Perspectives on Criminal Law* London: Cavendish Publishing.

Lacey, N., Wells, C. and Meure, D. (1990) *Reconstructing Criminal Law* London: Weidenfeld Paperbacks.

Leader-Elliott, I. (1997) 'Passion and Insurrection in the Law of Sexual Provocation' in Naffine, N. and Owens, R. (eds) *Sexing the Subject of Law* London: Sweet & Maxwell.

Letherby, G. (2003) *Feminist Research in Theory and Practice* Milton Keynes: Open University Press.

Lloyd, A. (1995) *Doubly Deviant, Doubly Damned* Harmondsworth: Penguin.

Marks, L. and Van den Bergh, T. (1990) *Ruth Ellis: A Case of Diminished Responsibility?* London: Penguin.

Masciola, A.L. (2002) '"The Unfortunate Maid Exemplified": Elizabeth Canning and Representations of Infanticide in Eighteenth-Century England' in Jackson, M. (ed.) *Infanticide: Historical Perspectives on Child Murder and Concealment 1550–2000* Aldershot: Ashgate.

Mathiesen, T. (2004) *Silently Silenced* Winchester: Waterside Press.

McNay, L. (1992) *Foucault and Feminism* Cambridge: Polity.

McNay, L. (2000) *Gender and Agency: Reconfiguring the Subject in Feminist and Social Theory* Cambridge: Polity Press.

McNay, L. (2004) 'Situated Intersubjectivity', in Marshall, B. and Witz, A. (eds) *Engendering the Social: Feminist Encounters with Sociological Theory* Maidenhead: Open University Press.

McRobbie, A. (2009) *The Aftermath of Feminism: Gender, Culture and Social Change* London: Sage.

Messing, J.T. and Heeren, J.W. (2009) 'Gendered Justice: Domestic Homicide and the Death Penalty' *Feminist Criminology* 4(2), 170–88.

Minkes, J. and Vanstone, M. (2006) 'Gender, Race and the Death Penalty: Lessons from Three 1950s Murder Trials' *Howard Journal* 45(4), 403–20.

Moody, S.R. (1995) 'Images of Women: Sentencing in Sexual Assault Cases in Scotland' in Bridgeman, J. and Millns, S. (eds) *Law and Body Politics* Aldershot: Dartmouth.

Morris, A. (1987) *Women, Crime and Criminal Justice* Oxford: Basil Blackwell.

Morris, A. and Wilczynski, A. (1993) 'Rocking the Cradle: Mothers Who Kill Their Children' in Birch, H. (ed.) *Moving Targets* London: Virago.

Morrissey, B. (2003) *When Women Kill* London: Routledge.

Munro, V. (2007) *Law and Politics at the Perimeter* Oxford: Hart Publishing.

Naffine, N. (1990) *Law & the Sexes* London: Allen & Unwin.

Naughton, M. (2007) *Rethinking Miscarriages of Justice* London: Palgrave.

Nicholson L.J. (ed.) (1990) *Feminism/Postmodernism* London: Routledge.

Nicolson, D. (2000) 'What the Law Giveth, it also Taketh Away: Female-Specific Defences to the Criminal Liability' in Nicolson, D. and Bibbings, L. (eds) *Feminist Perspectives on Criminal Law* London: Cavendish Publishing.

Nicolson, D. and Sanghwi, R. (1993) 'Battered Women and Provocation: The Implications of R. v Ahluwalia' *Criminal Law Review* October, 725–38.

Nobles, R. and Schiff, D. (2004) 'A Story of Miscarriage: Law in the Media' *Journal of Law and Society* 31(2), 221–44.

Norrie, A. (2001/2006) *Crime, Reason and History* Cambridge: Cambridge University Press.

Norrie, A. (2010) 'The Coroners and Justice Act 2009 – Partial Defences to Murder: (1) Loss of Control' *Criminal Law Review* 4, 275–89.

O'Donovan, K. (1985) *Sexual Divisions in Law* London: Weidenfeld & Nicolson.

O'Donovan, K. (1991) 'Defences for Battered Women Who Kill' *Journal of Law and Society* 18(2), 219–39.

O'Donovan, K. (1993) Law's Knowledge: The Judge, The Expert, The Battered Woman and Her Syndrome' *Journal of Law and Society* 20(4), 427–37.

O'Neill, R. (2014) 'Whither Critical Masculinity Studies? Notes on Inclusive Masculinity Theory, Postfeminism, and Sexual Politics' *Men and Masculinities*, 1–21.

Phoenix, J. and Oerton, S. (2005) *Illicit and Illegal: Sex, Regulation and Social Control* Cullompton: Willan Publishing.

Pitch, T. (1995) 'Feminist Politics, Crime, Law and Order in Italy' in Rafter, N.H. and Heidensohn, F. (eds) *International Feminist Perspectives in Criminology* Buckingham: Open University Press.

Pratt, J. and Gilligan, G. (2004) 'Introduction: Crime, Truth and Justice – Official Inquiry and the Production of Knowledge' in Gilligan, G. and Pratt, J. (eds) *Crime, Truth and Justice: Official Inquiry, Discourse, Knowledge* Cullompton: Willan Publishing.

Purkiss, D. (1996) *The Witch in History* London: Routledge.

Raitt, F.E. and Zeedyk, M.S. (2004) 'Mothers on Trial: Discourses of Cot Death and Munchausen's Syndrome by Proxy' *Feminist Legal Studies* 12, 257–78.

Rose, J. (1993) *Why War?* Oxford: Blackwell Publishers

Rose, J., Panter, S. and Wilkinson, T. (1997) *Innocents* London: Fourth Estate.

Royal Commission on Capital Punishment 1949–1953 Report.

Sachs, A. (1976) 'The Myth of Judicial Neutrality: The Male Monopoly Cases' in Carlen, P. (ed.) *The Sociology of Law* Keele University: Sociological Review Monograph 23.

Sagan, C. (1981) *Cosmos* London: MacDonald Futura Publishers.

Sawicki, J. (1991) *Disciplining Foucault* London: Routledge.

Segal, L. (1990) *Slow Motion* London: Virago.

Showalter, E. (1987) *The Female Malady* London: Virago.

Simon, J.K. (1971) 'A Conversation with Michel Foucault' *Partisan Review*, 192–201.

Smart, B. and Smart, C. (eds) (1978) *Women, Sexuality and Social Control* London: Routledge & Kegan Paul.

Smart, C. (1976) *Women, Crime and Criminology* London: Routledge & Kegan Paul.

Smart, C. (1989) *Feminism and the Power of Law* London: Routledge.

Smart, C. (1990) 'Feminist Approaches to Criminology or Postmodern Woman Meets Atavistic Man' in Gelsthorpe, L. and Morris, A. (eds) *Feminist Perspectives in Criminology* Milton Keynes: Open University Press. Also in Smart, C. (1995) *Law, Crime and Sexuality* London: Sage.

Smart, C. (ed.) (1992) *Regulating Womanhood* London: Routledge.

Smart, C. (1995) *Law, Crime and Sexuality* London: Sage.

Smart, C., Hockey, J. and James, A. (eds) (2014) *The Craft of Knowledge: Experiences of Living with Data* Basingstoke: Palgrave Macmillan.

Smith, D.E. (1987) *The Everyday World as Problematic* Milton Keynes: Open University Press.

Spender, D. (1980) *Man Made Language* London: Routledge & Kegan Paul.

Spensky, M. (1992) 'Producers of Legitimacy: Homes for Unmarried Mothers in the 1950s' in Smart, C. (ed.) *Regulating Womanhood* London: Routledge.

Springhall, J. (1987) 'Building Character in the British Boy: The Attempt to Extend Christian Manliness to Working-Class Adolescents, 1880 to 1914' in Mangan, J.A. and Walwin, J. (eds) *Manliness and Morality: Middle-Class Masculinity in Britain and America 1800–1940* Manchester: Manchester University Press.

Stanko, E. and Scully, A. (1996) 'Retelling the Tale: The Emma Humphreys Case' in Myers, A. and Wight, S. (eds) *No Angels* London: Pandora.

Stanley, L. and Wise, S. (1983) *Breaking Out* London: Routledge.

Stanley, L. and Wise, S. (1993) *Breaking Out Again: Feminist Ontology and Epistemology* London: Routledge.

Steedman, C. (2014) 'Living with the Dead' in Smart, C., Hockey, J. and James, A. (eds) *The Craft of Knowledge: Experiences of Living with Data* Basingstoke: Palgrave Macmillan.

Strange, C. (2003) 'Masculinities, Intimate Femicide and the Death Penalty in Australia 1890–1920' *British Journal of Criminology* 48, 310–39.

Svensson, B. (1997) 'The Power of Biography: Criminal Policy, Prison Life, and the Formation of Criminal Identities in the Swedish Welfare State' in Reed-Danahay, D. (ed.) *Auto/Ethnography* Oxford: Berg.

Tosh, J. (2004) 'Hegemonic Masculinity and the History of Gender' in Dudink, S., Hagermann, K. and Tosh, J. (eds) *Masculinities in Politics and War* Manchester: Manchester University Press.

Ussher, J. (1989) *The Psychology of the Female Body* London: Routledge.

Ussher, J. (1991) *Women's Madness* Hemel Hempstead: Harvester Wheatsheaf.

Walklate, S. (2007) *Imagining the Victim of Crime* Maidenhead: McGraw-Hill/Open University Press.

Ward, T. (1999) 'The Sad Subject of Infanticide: Law, Medicine and Child Murder 1860–1938' *Social & Legal Studies* 8(2), 163–80.

Ward, T. (2002) 'Legislating for Human Nature: Legal Responses to Infanticide, 1860–1938' in Jackson, M. (ed.) *Infanticide: Historical Perspectives on Child Murder and Concealment 1550–2000* Aldershot: Ashgate.

Ward, T. (2004) 'Experts, Juries, and Witch-Hunts: From Fitzjames Stephen to Angela Cannings' *Journal of Law and Society* 31(3), 369–86.

Wessling, M.N. (1994) 'Infanticide Trials and Forensic Medicine: Wurttemberts 1747–93' in Clark, M. and Crawford, C. (eds) *Legal Medicine in History* Cambridge: Cambridge University Press.

Wheelwright, J. (2002) '"Nothing in Between": Modern Cases of Infanticide' in Jackson, M. (ed.) Infanticide: *Historical Perspectives on Child Murder and Concealment 1550–2000* Aldershot: Ashgate.

Wilczynski, A. (1991) 'Images of Women Who Kill Their Infants: The Mad and the Bad' *Criminal Justice* 2, 71–88.

Worrall, A. (1990) *Offending Women* London: Routledge.
Worrall, A. (2002) 'Rendering Women Punishable: The Making of a Penal Crisis' in Carlen, P. (ed.) *Women and Punishment* Cullompton: Willan Publishing.
Yuval-Davis, N. (2006) 'Intersectionality and Feminist Politics' *European Journal of Women's Studies* 1(3), 193–209.
Yuval-Davis, N. (2011) *The Politics of Belonging: Intersectional Contestations* London: Sage.

National Archives

ASSI 81/64
DPP2/2430/23271
HO144/1581/323447
HO144/1749/419784
HO144/3148
HO144/3434
HO144/4526
HO144/6012
HO144/11692
HO291/235
HO291/236
PCOM 8/231
PCOM 8/242
PCOM 8/300
PCOM 8/5

Newspapers

Boseley, S. and Dyer, C. (2004) 'Call for Change in Baby Death Inquiries' *Guardian* 7 September p. 6.
Chapman, J. and Broster, P. (2003) 'Six Killer Mums to Be Freed' *Daily Express* 31 January pp. 1–7.
Cowan, R. (2004) 'Call for the Overhaul of Expert Testimony' *Guardian* 30 November p. 9.
Doward, J. (2005) 'Parents Demand Gag on Cot Death Doctor's Lectures' *Observer* 16 January.
Durham Chronicle 17 November 1916.
Dyer, C. (2005) 'Pathologist in Sally Clark Case Loses Accreditation' *Guardian* 3 December.
Evening Mail 13 November 1916.
Evening News 14 April 1926.
Frith, M. (2003) 'Mothers Convicted of Killing Babies May Get Case Review' *Independent* 12 December.
Glendinning, L. (2007) 'Sally Clark's Death "Probably Natural Causes"' *Guardian* 20 March.
Guardian 12 September 2003.
Guardian 18 February 2006.
Guardian 2 May 2008.

Guardian 24 November 2010.
Laville, S. (2006) 'Murder Cases Review after Expert Criticised' *Guardian* 1 November.
Lawrence Beech, B. (2003) Honorary Chair, Association for Improvements in the Maternity Services, 'The Lessons of a Shameful Trial' *Independent* 13 June.
News of the World 18 April 1926.
News of the World 27 June 1926.
Orr, D. (2003) 'Too Much Faith in Bad Science, Too Little Humanity' *Independent* 12 December.
Sweeney, J. (2003) 'Cot Deaths and Justice' *Observer* 15 June.
Sweeney, J. and Law, B. (2003) 'Gene Find Casts Doubt on Double "Cot Death" Murders' *Observer* 15 July.
Surrey Advertiser and County Times 3 December 1910.
Taylor, M. (2003) 'Profile: Expert with Controversial Theory' *Guardian* 11 December.
Vasager, J. and Allison, R. (2003) 'How Cot Deaths Shattered Mother's Dreams' *Guardian* 12 June.
Wardrop, M. (2009) 'Husband Guilty of Killing Vodafone Executive Wife after Affair' *Telegraph* 29 October.

Websites and Other Media

BBC1 *Ruth Ellis: A Life for a Life* broadcast 28 November 1999.
BBC News UK 'Families want Pathologist Freddy Patel Public Inquiry' 6 September 2012.
BBC News UK 22 November 2007.
Campbell, K. and Walker, C. (undated) 'Medical Mistakes and Miscarriages of Justice: Perspectives on the Experiences in England and Wales', available at: www.atterneygeneral.jus.gov.on.ca/.../Campbell_Walker.
File on Four broadcast 2 July 2002, Reporter: John Sweeney. Transcript available at: www.sallyclark.org.uk/FileonFour.html.
Hill, R. (2005) Reflections on the cot death cases in *Significance* 2(1) pp. 13–15; available on http:www.cse.salford.ac.uk/staff/RHill/Reflections.
Osborne, G. (2004) in *Parliamentary Debate on Family Court Cases* 24 February. Transcript available at: http://sallyclark.org.uk/Parliament0204.html.
Royal Statistical Society 23 October 2001 (News Release).

Cases

Ellis v. *R* (2003) EWCA Crim 3556.
Judgment *R* v. *Sally Clark* (2000) Case No: 1999/07495/Y3.
Judgment *R* v. *Sally Clark* (2003) *EWCA Crim 1020*, Case No: 200203824 Y3.
The Queen v. *Sally Clark*, Skeleton Argument (Clare Montgomery QC) 2002/3824/Y3.

Index

abortion 53
adultery 79, 90
agency 4, 25, 26, 29–33, 59, 62, 66, 76, 84, 92, 94, 119, 120
alcohol consumption 48, 113, 119
alternative truth 2, 3, 5, 8, 12, 13, 14, 20, 22, 23, 25, 37, 39, 44, 48–51, 57–8, 61, 69, 71, 73, 74, 91, 93, 97, 123
Aluwalia, K. 88

Batt, J. 103, 117
Battered Woman Syndrome (BWS) 76, 81, 82, 84, 92, 93
Blakely, D. 76, 77, 82
Boxhall, F. 58–61, 129

Cain, M. 3, 10, 12, 15, 18, 20, 37, 39, 44, 48
Calvert, L. 4, 6, 33, 34, 36–43, 46, 49, 52, 61, 68, 69, 95, 110, 126
Cannings, A. 23 f/n 1, 35, 98, 98 f/n 1, 115, 117, 123
Care of Next Infant programme (CONI) 99, 108
chivalry thesis 1
Clark, C. 98, 99, 100, 102, 105–9
Clark, H. 99–109, 115,
Clark, Sally 5, 7, 23 f/n 1, 97–9, 102–5, 109–10, 112–15, 117–24, 126
Clark, Stephen 98, 99, 105, 108, 112, 121, 122, 123, 123 f/n 9
Collier, R. 26
Collins, Mr Justice 123
Comack 13, 15, 20, 57, 65
Common Law 79, 80, 86
Connell, R. W. 24, 27, 28, 29–30, 64, 72, 73, 128
Cook, A. 67–73
Coroners and Justice Act (2009) 95
Crabtree, F. 46, 47, 49
Criminal Cases Review Commission (CCRC) 97, 105, 117, 122
crisis of legitimacy 49, 95, 109
Cussen, D. 77, 78, 81, 92, 93

death penalty 1, 6, 7, 36, 55, 70, 73
Destroying and Murthering of Bastard Children Act (1623) 54
Devlin, Lord 87
diminished responsibility 78, 79, 80, 82, 84, 91, 92, 94–5
domestic violence 41, 83, 89, 91,128, 129
double standard 2, 31, 34, 72
doubly deviant 34, 38, 48, 110

Ellis, R. 6, 33, 75–8, 78 f/n 2, 79–81, 83, 85, 86–9, 91–6, 119, 125, 130
emphasised femininity 27, 28, 31
Enlightenment 9, 10, 11, 13, 16, 17, 18, 21, 22, 34, 82, 109, 121
equity studies 10
essentialism 13, 28
execution 6, 39, 44, 50, 54, 73, 75, 77, 78 f/n 2, 81
expert knowledge 5, 7, 20, 22, 23, 24, 25, 55, 56, 59, 71, 92, 97, 98, 109–11, 113–14, 117, 119–24, 126

Faith, K. 2, 3, 6, 37
feminist empiricism 10
feminist epistemology 3, 4, 5, 6, 9, 10–14, 20, 33, 36, 37, 50–2, 72, 95
feminist standpoint *see* standpoint feminism

File on Four (2002) 116
Foucauldian 21, 93, 120, 126
Foucault, M. 21, 22, 23, 29, 36, 49, 50, 110, 111, 111 f/n 5, 112, 113, 114, 122, 125, 126, 130 f/n 1
Fraser, N. 20, 30, 127
Frobisher, J. 41, 42

gender role expectations 34, 110
gender-blindness 10
General Medical Council (GMC) 118, 123

Harding, S. 9, 13, 16, 17, 18
Havers, Mr Justice 77, 80, 81
hegemonic masculinity 27–30, 64, 67, 72, 73, 128
heteropatriarchy 13, 18, 30, 66
hidden silencing (*see also* 'silent silencing') 94, 95, 96, 130
hierarchy of knowledge 1, 5, 35, 48, 51, 83
'history from below' 125, 126
Home Office 38, 39, 42, 43, 44–50, 57, 59, 60, 64, 65–72, 98, 122, 123, 124
Homicide Act 1957 79, 80
Humphrys, E. 84

ideological mystification 6, 51
illegitimacy 43
inclusive masculinity 29, 30
industrial revolution 26
intersectionality 19–20

judges of normality 21, 35, 110
judicial misogyny 43, 48
Judicial Studies Board 117

knowledge production 4, 11, 16, 20, 23, 24, 25, 34, 37, 38, 44, 50, 51, 82, 83, 85, 91, 93, 110, 121

Lord, D. 58
Loss of Control Defence 2010 85, 88, 91, 95

Mansfield, M. 79, 81, 82, 86
manslaughter 58, 77, 78f/n 2, 79, 84, 129
masculinity 5, 21, 25–30, 33, 60, 61, 64, 67, 72, 73, 74, 82, 128
Masset, L. 6, 43 f/n 5, 55 f/n 2, 73
Mathiesen, T. 76, 91, 92, 94
McRobbie, A. 127
Meadow, Sir Roy 98 f/n 1, 102–5, 108, 109, 111, 113, 114–18, 121, 123
'Meadow's Law' 111, 114
Medical Practitioners Tribunal 122
mental illness 70, 71
miscarriage of justice 5, 6, 7, 25, 35, 97, 108, 109, 123, 124, 126, 130
Modified Glasgow Coma Score 116
Morrissey, B. 31
motherhood 2, 26, 27, 34, 41, 48, 53, 57, 62, 120, 126
Munchausen's Syndrome by Proxy (MSbP) 103, 111, 116, 117 f/n 8, 118

Naughton, M. 5

O'Donovan 25, 32, 50, 87, 92, 120
official discourse 2, 4, 5, 7, 12, 17, 20, 21, 22, 23, 25, 34, 35, 36, 37–8, 41, 42, 44, 47, 49, 50, 51, 53, 58, 61, 72, 73, 90, 97, 114, 120, 121, 126, 129
official statistics 1

Patel, F. 122, 123
Patel, T. 117, 118, 121, 123
pathology 2, 55, 59, 63, 66, 71, 74, 105
patriarchy 14, 15, 20, 24, 27, 28, 50, 64
phallocentric 5, 9, 11, 20, 21, 23, 24, 25, 29, 31, 32, 33, 34, 54, 62, 64, 85, 87, 88, 89, 90, 91, 92, 93, 110, 120
phallocentric law 25, 29, 31, 33, 87, 89, 91, 92, 93
politics of difference 15, 16, 24
politics of naming 9
Pollak, O. 1
Poor Law (1833 and 1844) 54
postmodern feminism 11, 13, 14–20, 24, 30
presumption of innocence 49, 111, 113
professional misconduct 109, 118, 123
provocation 76, 77, 78, 79, 80–1, 83, 85–7, 89–90, 92, 95–6

Raitt and Zeedyk 98, 112
rationality 4, 21, 22, 27, 30, 31, 32, 35, 49, 59, 63, 70, 74, 83, 95, 109
regimes of truth 2, 3, 93
Rich, A. 2

Royal College of Paediatrics and Child Health 111, 114
Royal College of Pathologists 123
Royal College of Physicians 114
Royal Commission on Capital Punishment 1949–1953 Report 1, 2
Royal Statistical Society 115

'silent silencing' 76, 91, 93
Smart, C. 20, 21, 28, 32, 41, 50, 53, 54, 56, 73, 96, 130
social class 27, 44, 45, 55, 61
social order 6, 7, 21, 24, 25, 26, 27, 28, 30, 31, 32, 33, 51, 54, 55, 56, 57, 61, 64, 66–7, 72, 74, 89, 91, 92, 94, 110, 119, 127, 128, 129, 130
standpoint feminism 3, 11–18, 19, 20, 22, 24, 26, 36, 37, 44
Stephen, Sir Fitzjames 74
Stevenson, M. 77
subjugated knowledge 2, 3, 4, 12, 16, 22, 23, 24, 25, 34, 36, 39–41, 44, 48, 49–51, 53, 110, 120, 121, 126, 129
Sudden Infant Syndrome (SIDS) 98, 99, 101, 102, 108, 115
Sudden Unexpected Death in Infancy Report (SUDI) 123
Sweeney, J. 97, 116, 118

theoretical reflexivity 3, 4, 12, 18, 37, 48
Thornton, S. 84, 88
Tomlinson, I. 122
transgressive criminology 3

Vaccine Damage Payment Act (1979) 115

Waterhouse, L. 37, 41, 49, 126
Williams, A. 98, 99, 100, 101, 102, 104, 105, 106–8, 109, 112, 118, 122, 123
Wilson, H. 58, 61–3, 67, 72

Yuval-Davis 19, 20

Zellick, G. 117

www.ingramcontent.com/pod-product-compliance
Ingram Content Group UK Ltd.
Pitfield, Milton Keynes, MK11 3LW, UK
UKHW011019180926
475701UK00004B/832
9780367596361